Economics Made Easy

3ʳᵈ Edition

By

Les Livingstone[1]

1Les Livingstone MBA, Ph.D., CPA (NY & TX) is an MBA Program Director
and professor in economics, finance & accounting at the University of
Maryland University College, a leading online university with 100,000
students including 3,000 MBA students.

Economics Made Easy 3rd edition Copyright 2013 by Les Livingstone

Dedication

To Trudy, Robert and Amy, with love.

Preface to 3rd Edition

Why another economics book? There must be thousands of books on economics. So what excuse is there for adding yet another book to this huge pile?

Most of the other economics books are lengthy, or loaded with mathematics or technical jargon, or just plain dull to read. Economics wasn't called "the dismal science" for nothing.

This book is very short. It is not at all mathematical or technical, and it is lively to read. It still includes all the important basic ideas and concepts of economics. But it explains them in words that are easy to understand. One might call it an executive summary of mainline economics.

I think that's a pretty good excuse for yet another book on economics.

Les Livingstone

Economics Made Easy 3rd edition Copyright 2013 by Les Livingstone

Table of Contents

Chapter 1: Introduction

"The first lesson of economics is scarcity: there is never enough of anything to fully satisfy all those who want it.

The first lesson of politics is to disregard the first lesson of economics".

Thomas Sowell

Scarce Resources.

We live in a world of scarce resources, and unlimited desires. If resources were unlimited, no one would ever starve, or be homeless, or wear tattered clothing. Every person would have plenty to eat, plenty of shelter, and plenty of clothes. That may be true for some of us. But it is only a distant dream for much of the world's population. Many people go hungry, have little or no shelter, and wear only rags.

We also live in a world of unlimited desires. Even the most fortunate and affluent among us have less than they desire, no matter how wealthy they may be. For example, the top executives of Enron were rich, almost beyond belief, but still wanted yet more than they already had.

In the developing nations of the world poverty is widespread, and is the rule rather than the exception. The U.S. is the most prosperous nation in the world. But there are still poor people in the U.S. As Tevye the dairyman in *Fiddler on the Roof* said: "It's no shame to be poor. But it's no great honor either. Would it spoil some vast eternal plan if I were a wealthy man?"

In short, scarcity of resources is the usual state of affairs all over the world. Scarcity of resources exists widely in the developing nations, a n d still persists, although much less widely, in the wealthiest nations. In poorer nations, the scarcity of resources and prevalence of poverty is often accompanied by violence and brutality, with the strong robbing the weak, and marauding gangs of bandits living off crime. Warlords oppress the wretched population, and vicious dictators ruthlessly strip their helpless subjects of whatever pitifully little they earn from endless toil, in order for these predators to live in the lap of luxury, and to build up huge balances in Swiss banks.

Social Order and Prosperity

We may ask: what leads to social order and widespread prosperity in nations like the U.S. and other industrialized nations rather than the poverty, brutality and chaos that prevail in less fortunate countries? In other words, how do some nations advance from the scarcest resources and deepest poverty to less scarcity and increased prosperity? The answer is operation of the rule of law, including enforcement of secure property rights. The rule of law and secure property rights enable people to cooperate in the free and mutually beneficial exchange of goods and services, because:

1. The environment is orderly, and largely free of crime and corruption;
2. The strong cannot just seize goods belonging to the weak;
3. People are willing to work hard when they can enjoy the fruits of their labors without fearing to be robbed;
4. Commitments and contracts can be relied upon.
5. Trade is stimulated when people have clear title to goods, and can transfer clear title when they sell those goods to buyers;

The Rule of Law and Secure Property Rights

The rule of law and secure property rights provide freedom from intimidation by violent criminals and by predatory dictators. This freedom allows people to make whatever choices they may wish, so long as their choices are within the law and respectful of the persons and property rights of their fellow citizens.

Free choices, which are within the law and which are respectful of property rights, result in mutually beneficial trading between individuals. Exchanges of goods and services for money are motivated by each person's pursuit of self-interest. With free choice, either the buyer or the seller would reject the transaction unless they benefitted from it. So all transactions under free choice must benefit both the buyer and the seller – otherwise these transactions would not take place. Self- interest guides the choices, and trade-offs that we make. Individual choices, motivated by self-interest, result in an efficient economy that:

1. Automatically and spontaneously coordinates itself (Adam Smith's "invisible hand").

2. Creates collective wealth with every voluntary trade.

In short, economics is the study of individual choice guided by self-interest. Individual choice guided by self-interest, in turn, creates collective wealth, so long as the rule of law with secure property rights is effectively enforced. That is why operation of the rule of law, including enforcement of secure property rights, leads to social order and widespread prosperity. By the same token, absence of the rule of law, and enforcement of secure property rights, leads to poverty, violence and brutality.

When we use the term "self-interest" we do not mean greed. Greed refers to gluttony, self-indulgence, avarice, or covetousness. Greed implies selfish behavior that ignores or rides recklessly over the rights of others. Greed is basically unethical behavior which fails to recognize or respect the interests of other people. In sharp contrast, self-interest involves pursuing one's own best interests, while recognizing and respecting the rights of others. For example, a store owner may well wish to maximize store profits. But the store will not attract and retain customers if customers are short-changed, or overcharged, or misinformed, or deceived, or unfairly treated. So long as the store owner maximizes store profits without treating customers deceitfully, then that store owner will be successful in pursuing his or her self-interest. But if that store owner falls guilty to greed and indulges in selfish behavior that ignores or rides roughshod over the rights of customers, then success will be short-lived. Therefore it is extremely important to distinguish between self-interest, which is legitimate and ethical, versus greed which is neither legitimate nor ethical. Self-interest is the basis of prosperity for all, at the expense of none. Greed is the basis of prosperity for the few, at the expense of the many.

Perhaps we should add that businesspeople are sometimes accused of "greed." This accusation probably includes a kernel of truth, in that some businesspeople may well be greedy. However, that does not mean that all – or even a majority – of businesspeople are greedy, because:

1. Plainly it is hardly likely that all greedy people go into business, while all righteous people go into government;
2. More likely, people are just people – some may be moral and some might be greedy. So probably there are both moral and greedy people in all walks of life, regardless of whether they work in business, in government, or elsewhere.
3. In any case, "greed" is just a <u>motive</u>. It cannot be exercised unless there is also <u>opportunity</u> to cheat potential victims. Competition reduces the opportunity to cheat potential victims, so perhaps finding potential victims to cheat is less likely in business than in other fields, because competition tends to be more prevalent in business than in other fields.

Therefore it seems that accusing only businesspeople of "greed" is more likely to signify a lack of thought than an actual state of affairs.

Efficiency

We used the term "efficient" above. What do we mean by "efficient?" When engineers use the term "efficient" they mean that output is greater than input. For example, if a process produces more energy than the energy required to operate that process, then the process is efficient. The energy output exceeds the energy input.

In economics, the term "efficient" means something similar. For example, when a purchaser and a seller engage in a transaction, each one gains – otherwise they would not enter into the transaction. Both purchaser and seller are better off after the transaction than before. The inputs into the transaction are the object being sold by the seller, and the money price being paid by the purchaser. The outputs of the transaction are also the same: namely, the object sold by the seller, and the money price paid by the purchaser. So the inputs seem equal to the outputs.

Although the physical nature of the inputs is identical to the physical nature of the outputs, the economic value of the outputs is greater than the economic value of the inputs, because the buyer values the object more highly than the seller did, and the seller values the money more highly than the purchaser did. Both buyer and seller are better off. Their benefits exceed their costs, and the individual wealth of the buyer and the seller have both increased. Therefore the transaction is efficient.

Another term that economists use for an efficient transaction is Pareto-efficient[2]. Pareto-efficient means that all parties are better-off and none is worse-off. Further, a transaction is Pareto-optimal if there is no other arrangement that can make any party better-off, without making any party worse-off.

To summarize, every voluntary transaction is efficient (or Pareto-efficient) because every party is better off after the transaction than before. An economy consists of a great many different transactions. If all of these transactions are free exchanges, then each is efficient. Given that every transaction is efficient, then the entire economy must also be efficient. And that, in a nutshell, is why free economies are the most efficient form of economic organization.

Notice that economic efficiency is based upon self-interest, but not upon greed. Self-interest is Pareto-efficient, whereas greed is not.

Free Markets and Prosperity

Free markets under the rule of law are the foundation of economic prosperity. Free markets provide for unrestricted flows of human and non-human capital, and the rule of law protects private property and the rights of individuals. In researching the factors that determined per capita income across countries, Richard Roll and John Talbott found that government regulation accounted for more than 80 percent of the variation of gross national income per capita between countries[3]. The following three factors had the

---

2 Pareto is an Italian economist named Vilfredo Pareto.(1848-1923).

3 Richard Roll and John Talbott, "Why Developing Countries Just Aren't," www.worlddevelopmentnow.com/id21.htm Also see: Robert J. Barro, Determinants of Economic Growth: A Cross-Country Empirical Study (Cambridge, Mass.: MIT Press, 1997); Robert Cooter, "The Rule of State Law and the Rule-of-Law State: Economic Analysis of the Legal Foundations of Development," in Edgardo Buscaglia, William Ratliff, and Robert Cooter, eds.,

greatest significance in explaining those variations:

- "<u>property rights</u>," described as the strength of the rule of law and the independence of the judiciary;

- "<u>regulations</u>," representing the regulatory burden on businesses;

- "<u>black market</u>," regarded as the amount of unofficial or illicit economic activity.

In short, the Roll-Talbott study explains that people invest, work, and consume most efficiently where regulatory barriers are lowest and, most crucially, where property rights are securely protected. In order to encourage permanent investment and sustainable economic growth, governments must follow honest policies, minimize regulations, and - most importantly - guarantee the security of property rights. Without the rule of law, societies cannot prevent private abuse and public corruption.

<u>Necessary Conditions</u>

Strictly speaking, all of what we have said above depends on some crucial factors. We have implicitly assumed that the following conditions are true:

- There are many buyers and sellers of each kind of goods and services, so that no single buyer or seller is big enough or powerful enough to affect the market price of any of the goods or services that are being bought or sold. In other words, all buyers and sellers are "price takers" as opposed to "price makers."

Law and Economics of Development (Greenwich, Conn.: JAI Press, 1997);
Hernando de Soto, The Other Path: The Invisible Revolution in the Third World (New York: Harper and Row, 1989). Also see
http://muse.jhu.edu/login?uri=/journals/journal_of_democracy/v014/14.3roll.html

- Sellers cannot collude formally or informally to restrict supply or raise prices, and buyers cannot collude to form purchasing groups or associations that can pressure sellers into granting discounts or other privileges to their members, but deny those advantages to buyers who are not members.

- All buyers and sellers are fully informed about the facts relevant to their transactions; for example, that the buyer of a used car knows as much about its condition as the seller, and that an applicant for a bank loan has fully and truthfully disclosed his or her financial condition to the bank.

- That when we refer to a certain good or service, all sellers are offering the same good or service. For example, if we are analyzing the market for desktop personal computers, then we are referring to personal computers that are identical or homogenous, such as Windows 8 laptops with 8 gigabytes of RAM, 800 gigabyte hard disks, and 24x CD/DVD/RW optical drives. In other words, we must compare apples with apples, and not apples with oranges (for users of Apple computers, no pun intended).

- Transaction costs are zero. For example, we assume that all buyers have equal access to all sellers, so that no buyer has to travel more miles to access a seller than any other buyer. And that no seller requires buyers to pay a membership fee in order to buy, or offers free shipping when other sellers charge for shipping.

These conditions create what economists refer to as "perfect competition." Perfect competition does not exist when there is only one seller (monopoly) or one buyer (monopsony) or only a few sellers (oligopoly) or only a few buyers (oligopsony). In markets where monopoly, monopsony, oligopoly or oligopsony may apply, perfect competition does not prevail.

There are some markets where competition is perfect, or near-perfect. For example, in the U.S. common stocks are traded in a market that is virtually perfect, except perhaps for small variations in transaction costs because very large lots of stocks are traded at lower brokerage fees per share than very small lots of stocks.

Most markets tend to be in a grey area – not fully perfect, but not quite subject to monopoly, monopsony, oligopoly or oligopsony either. At first glance, this seems confusing, because it's a grey area where nothing is black or white. However, there are two factors that help to reduce the confusion.

- First, monopoly, monopsony, oligopoly or oligopsony tends to be fleeting and transitory in nature. Markets are dynamic, and ever-shifting. For example, at one time U.S. auto markets were dominated by the Big 3 auto makers: General Motors, Ford and Chrysler. Today, U.S. auto markets are much more competitive, given the substantial market penetration achieved by Japanese, Korean, German, and other auto makers such as Toyota, Honda, Hyundai, BMW, and Mercedes. Another example is the rapid rise and speedy success of newer companies such as Google, Amazon and Whole Foods. In our dynamic economy, no monopoly, monopsony, oligopoly or oligopsony is safe. There are always unexpected potential competitors and new technology around the corner to depose any current monopoly, monopsony, oligopoly or oligopsony.

- The second equalizing factor is the prevalence of substitutes. The vast majority of goods and services have substitutes. Some substitutes are very similar in nature to the subject good. Other substitutes may be less similar, but sufficiently similar to blunt the impact of monopoly, monopsony, oligopoly or oligopsony. For example, consider satellite radio – which is mostly used for news and entertainment in autos.

At present there is only one supplier of satellite radio broadcasting. Is this a monopoly? The answer is a definite no, because there are many substitutes for news and entertainment in autos, such as AM radio, FM radio, HD radio, CD players, audio cassette players, and MP3 players. These substitutes severely limit the power of satellite radio to charge monopoly prices.

Forces Pushing Towards Competitive Markets.

In our dynamic economy no monopoly, monopsony, oligopoly or oligopsony is safe. Even if there are few potential competitors, very little new technology, and a lack of good substitutes, new threats to existing players can emerge from unexpected directions. A good example is the s e t b a c k to firms like Krispy Kreme Doughnuts delivered from low-carb, high-protein diets like t h e Atkins and South Beach diets. Some items that we grew up with have become extinct – like pay phones (killed by cell phones), CD players (killed by MP3 players) even movie theatres (being pushed hard by streaming online videos).

While perfect competition may not fully exist in many markets, there are powerful tendencies that continuously move most markets towards perfect competition. As a result, the assumptions underlying perfect competition may not be fully applicable all of the time, but are largely applicable most of the time. Therefore in countries like the U.S. markets tend to be reasonably free, and our economy tends to be reasonably efficient.

The U.S. economy is competitive. For example, of the original 30 stocks in the Dow Jones Industrial Index, only one is still in that index: General Electric Corporation. Of the companies in the Standard & Poors 500 Stock Index, about 10% turn over each year. Given that we live under the rule of law, with secure property rights, and are not subject to excessive government regulation, we are a very prosperous nation. In contrast, countries where the rule of law is largely or totally absent, where property rights are vague or insecure, and where government regulation is pervasive, tend to be mired in poverty. There are many examples of such poverty-stricken nations in Africa, in Asia, and in Latin America. These poor nations seem fated to remain stuck in poverty until they are able to establish the rule of law with secure property rights, and to significantly reduce excessive government regulation.

Competition is the Key

Why is actual or potential competition so essential for economic prosperity? Because it is actual or potential competition that:
1. Provides business the incentive to be efficient,
2. Encourages workers to do their best,
3. Rewards invention and innovation.

It is the lack of competition that largely accounts for the lack of efficiency in:
1. Socialist and communist economies,
2. Government operations, because politicians are spending taxpayers' money, rather than their own money, which is usually spent with more care than other peoples' money[1].
3. Crony capitalism, which substitutes political favoritism for economic efficiency,

Therefore in the interest of economic efficiency it is competition that government should facilitate, rather than competitors – which would favor crony capitalism rather than equal opportunity capitalism.

Economics and Politics

---

[1] There is a joke (of which we neither approve nor disapprove) that drunken sailors are more prudent than politicians because drunken sailors at least are spending their own money, rather than other peoples' money.

[2] Income is also referred to as "profit" or "earnings". Income consists of revenue less

Economics and politics are completely different from each other.

1. Economics is based upon logic and upon factual evidence. That is how we know that larger quantities of a good or a service are likely to be purchased at lower prices than at higher prices. And that is how economic principles are derived – everything is based on logic and on factual evidence. Economics is only about efficiency. It can analyze choices that tell us what alternative is most efficient. There are right and wrong answers in economics - so far as economic efficiency is concerned.

2. In contrast, politics is not based on logic and on factual evidence. Rather, politics is based on <u>values</u>. Values are not a matter of logic or factual evidence, but are inherent personal preferences. There are no right and wrong answers in politics, only different values. So no value can be better or worse than any other value. In politics, values matter much more than economic efficiency. These values may be things like patriotism, or environmentalism, or animal rights, or same-sex marriage, or egalitarianism, or collective versus individual decision-making.

So economics and politics are different and distinct from each other. Please bear in mind that this book deals only with economics, and never with politics. Nothing is about Democrat or Republican. So please do not regard anything as leaning towards either Democrat or Republican values – this book is strictly about economics and about efficiency, and not about values. So, there is no politics, and therefore no Democrat and no Republican anywhere in the book.

Chapter Summary

- Much of the world suffers from extreme scarcity of resources and deep poverty.
- How have some nations progressed towards less scarcity and greater prosperity? By means of the rule of law and secure property rights.
- Under the rule of law and secure property rights, people make free choices that increase individual and collective wealth.
- The result is a competitive and efficient economy, where trade makes everyone better off.

Discussion Questions

1. Jane Goodperson is very wealthy. She gives a donation of $100 million to the state university for a new building to house the business school, which will now be named The Jane Goodperson School of Business. To what extent do you think her donation is motivated by philanthropy or by self-interest?

2. Imagine that the fictional nation of Erewhon has an embassy in Washington DC. One day the ambassador of Erewhon to the U.S. is driving his car down K Street in Washington DC. at three times the speed limit. The car veers off the road and hits three people, killing two and severely injuring the third person. A policeman witnesses this tragedy, but refuses to issue a citation to the driver because the car has diplomatic license plates and the ambassador has diplomatic immunity. Does this indicate that the U.S. has a weakness in its rule of law, or is diplomatic immunity fully consistent with the operation of the rule of law in the United States?

3. Five hundred people live in a shabby, run-down section of Gotham City. The Gotham City Council is approached by a property developer who wants to tear down the shabby, run-down houses and build expensive condominiums in their place. The developer urges the Gotham City Council to take the shabby, run-down section under its power of eminent domain[4], so that he can tear down the shabby, neglected houses and build expensive condominiums in their place. The Gotham City Council will collect three times the amount of property taxes from the expensive condominium development than they are presently collecting from the residents of the shabby, run-down section of Gotham City. If the Gotham City Council exercises its power of eminent domain in this manner, is this a Pareto-efficient economic transaction? Is it justifiable under the concept of secure property rights?

4. Does the doctrine of self-interest mean that people seek money in order to gain more control over their lives, or to increase their ability to make free choices, or is it just plain greed?

5. The downtown is getting more and more crowded. It has become increasingly difficult to find a parking place. What should the city council do? Should it build free municipal parking garages? Should it build metered municipal parking garages? Or should it do nothing, and leave the problem alone?

6. Celebrities have set records such as the following:

a) Tiger Woods has more wins than any other currently active

---

4 Eminent domain is the right of a government to appropriate private property for public use, such as highway construction, usually with compensation to the owner.

PGA professional golfer.

b) The Williams sisters have won more Grand Slam titles than any other tennis professionals.

c) Cy Young has pitched more wins (511) than any other professional baseball pitcher.

d) Brett Favre has started more games as quarterback than any other NFL quarterback.

e) Meryl Streep has starred in more movies than most other actresses.

f) Tom Hanks has starred in more movies than most other actors.

Are these celebrities examples of greed?

Chapter 2: Specialization, Trade and Prosperity

"Specialization makes each person the more directly dependent upon the supplementary activities of all others."

Georg Simmel

Self Sufficient Living

As a child, I lived on a cattle ranch, where my parents kept dairy cattle, and also range-fed beef cattle. I vividly recall that we milked the cows, and produced regular milk, skim milk, buttermilk, butter, sweet cream, sour cream, and cream cheese, some for our own use, but most for sale. I remember my father dragging cows out of ditches, helping cows give birth, and even giving aspirin to sick animals, by putting powdered aspirin in a tube made of old newspaper. He put one end of the tube in the cow's mouth, and the other end in his own mouth. He used to joke that it was important to blow first in order to give the aspirin to the cow. If by any chance the cow blew first my father would swallow a king-size dose of aspirin, courtesy of the cow.

I remember growing our own vegetables and fruit, and providing our own meat and poultry from our ranch cattle and chickens. My mother used to put up endless amounts of canned meat and canned vegetables and canned fruit for our use during the winter. She also made dried fruit and beef jerky, left to dry on the roof under a cloth to protect it from the birds. We chopped our own wood for the stove and pumped water from the well for use in the house.

In short, we grew or made much of which we consumed. My parents worked from first light until dark outside the house, and often worked inside at night. There was always so much work to be done - even on weekends, because the cattle did not know that Saturdays, Sundays, and holidays were supposed to be days of rest and relaxation. They continued to fall into ditches, or to give birth, or to require feeding and milking on Saturdays, Sundays, and holidays just as if these were weekdays.

Despite all this self-sufficiency, we still had to buy many items we could not make by ourselves - such as pots, pans, shoes, clothes, tools, machinery and cars and trucks. And, despite all the hard work, my parents were not affluent. Being largely self-sufficient is satisfying in many ways. But while it may produce satisfaction, it does not produce material riches because it is not efficient. A jack of all trades is master of none. A jack of all trades is inherently inefficient. Self-sufficiency is the road to poverty.

Specialization

Specialization has long been known as being far more efficient than spreading one's abilities more widely. The famous economist, Adam Smith, wrote about specialization in his well-known example of a pin factory, where:

"One man draws out the wire, another straightens it, a third cuts it, a fourth points it, a fifth grinds it at the top for receiving the head; to make the head requires two or three distinct operations; to put it on is a peculiar business, to whiten the pins is another; it is even a trade by itself to put then into the paper...... "

Smith observed that ten specialized workers could produce 48,000 pins a day. One unspecialized worker performing all operations alone could make perhaps only 20 pins per day, and could not get anywhere close to the average output per worker of 4,800 pins per day.

None of us can make everything we need from scratch. Instead we specialize, often quite narrowly, in what we produce, and use our earnings to purchase the wide variety of ready-made goods and services that we use. Specialization enables each of us to exchange what we produce in order to acquire what others have produced.

Of course, we have come a long way from Adam Smith's pin factory. Yesterday, specialization meant becoming a physician, a dentist, a lawyer, an accountant or a physical therapist. Today it means becoming:

- Not just a physician, but perhaps a pediatrician, a spinal surgeon, a gynecologist, a nephrologist, an endocrinologist, or a dermatologist;
- Not just a dentist, but an endodontist, a periodontist or a dental implant specialist;
- Not just a lawyer, but a litigator, or a trust and estate lawyer, or a real estate attorney;
- Not just an accountant, but an auditor, a tax accountant, or a forensic accountant;
- Not just a physical therapist, but an edema physical therapist, a sports injury physical therapist, or a yoga physical therapist.

Once we become very narrowly specialized, we become increasingly dependent on supplying what we offer, and buying just about everything else that we consume. The more we specialize, the more dependent we become on selling what we produce and buying what we use. Economic activity basically consists of people making voluntary exchanges of property. People exchange property rights by trading away what they value less highly in order to obtain what they value more highly. Something that is more valuable to me may be less valuable to you. That would encourage me to buy it, and encourage you to sell it to me. And it is this difference in value from one person to another that gives rise to trade. Trade makes both parties better off. In other words, it creates wealth. Wealth is whatever people value. In consequence, value is subjective in nature. Value is in the eye of the beholder.

Wealth

To recap, some good or service may be either more or less valuable to one person than to another person. That leads those persons to exchange that particular good or service by means of a trade. Each party to an exchange makes a gain, which increases their wealth. All voluntary exchanges increase the wealth of each of the participants. So long as it is voluntary, then it is a win-win proposition - everyone wins, and no- one loses. Exchange generates wealth. Societies with clear property rights and few restrictions on trade become wealthier than societies without clear property rights and barriers to, or many restrictions on, trade. Specialization exists because of trade, and trade exists because of specialization.

Wealth is produced by trading. Trading arises from specialization, because specialization means buying from others rather than making everything ourselves. Also, specialization is more efficient than self-sufficiency, thus allowing us to become wealthier if we specialize, rather than being jacks of all trades, and masters of none. For trading to flourish, requires freedom from robbery by violent criminals and from coercion from predatory dictators. Free choice depends on the rule of law, including enforcement of secure property rights. In short, it is the rule of law, including enforcement of secure property rights that leads to economic prosperity.

Incidentally, wealth and income[2] are different from each other. Income is earned over a period, such as a month or a year. If you like, income is a flow, like a movie. For example, income may be $X,000 per year. Income may be consumed or saved. The portion of income that is saved may earn interest or dividends or capital gains.

---

[2] Income is also referred to as "profit" or "earnings". Income consists of revenue less related expenses incurred in the pursuit of revenue.

23

These savings plus interest or dividends or capital gains are wealth. If you like, wealth is a stock (namely a cumulative sum at a moment in time), like a still picture. For example, wealth may be the $Y,000 net worth of a business or a person or a business as of December 31, 20ZZ.

Again, we have confirmed what we found in Chapter 1: the rule of law, including secure property rights, is the foundation of economic prosperity. It is the rule of law, including secure property rates, that is the basis of exchange transactions, which arise from specialization, under competition, which produces efficiency, which creates prosperity.

Chapter Summary

- Specialization allows people to become more productive and more prosperous than if they were self-sufficient.
- The more specialized one becomes, the more one depends on others to supply one's needs.
- Trade flourishes by means of the rule of law and secure property rights.
- Under the rule of law and secure property rights, people are more able to specialize, compete, and make free choices that increase individual and collective wealth.
- The result is a competitive and efficient economy, where trade makes everyone better off.

Discussion Questions

1. Some people want to quit their jobs and move to the country in order to live a simpler life, growing their own food, making their own clothing, and in general getting back to nature. Is this an efficient economic choice? If yes, then how can it be efficient if those people lower their standard of living by no longer having automobiles, computers, cell phones, I-pods, or television sets? If no, are they making a decision that is contrary to their own self-interest?

2. Some people say that specialization can be carried too far. For example, is it carried too far when an ear-nose-and-throat physician specializes in only the left ear and left nostril?

3. Which people are likely to be more specialized:
   a. Those living in developing nations, or those living in industrialized nations?

b. Those living in cities or those living in the countryside?

c. Those living in temperate climates or those living in tropical climates?

4. As one becomes more specialized, so one becomes more dependent on other people, both as customers and also as suppliers. Does this mean that specialization increases our choices or narrows our choices? How does one make the trade-off between specialization and dependency?

5. How does specialization relate to the rule of law and secure property rights?

6. What is the relationship, if any, between specialization and self-interest?

Chapter 3: Demand for Goods and Services

As scarce as truth is, the supply has always been in excess of the demand.

Josh Billings

Desire versus Demand

First, we need to clarify what we mean by demand. Demand means the quantity of any particular good that people will buy at a given price. Notice that demand is not how much of a good that people need or desire. Needs or desires may be keenly felt, but do not necessarily lead to actual purchases of goods or services. As the saying goes: "if wishes were horses, then beggars would ride." People cannot buy what they cannot pay for. Therefore needs or desires are not effective demand. Effective demand means only the quantity is actually purchased.

Also notice that the quantity that people will purchase is not fixed. It varies according to the price. So, in economics, the quantity actually purchased is seldom (if ever) absolute. It tends to be relative, depending on price. This is very important to remember. In casual conversation, people often mention "demand" as if it is one fixed amount. They say, for example, that demand for Lexus autos is high, or that demand for less popular makes of autos is low. This may be fine for casual conversation, but it is too vague and not specific enough for serious discussion of economic principles.

The quantity demanded depends on the price because goods are scarce. If there was an unlimited supply of any particular good, everyone could have as much as they wanted, and there would be no-one willing to pay even a penny for that good. For example, generally we have all the air that we need to breathe. So air is free. But that changes if air becomes scarce. For example, if air pollution becomes intense, we may need to purchase surgical masks in order to breathe. Similarly, if one has difficulty breathing because of heart or lung deficiencies, then one becomes willing to pay for oxygen. So it is scarcity that drives price.

Rationing

Scarcity means there isn't enough of some good or service to satisfy everyone's desires. That makes rationing necessary. Rationing may be implemented by any of the following approaches:

- By **quotas** imposed by the government (for example, everyone gets one pair of shoes per year). This method was used by nations involved in World War Two, and by Soviet Russia and Communist in both times of war and of peace.

- By **favoritism or patronage**. Members of the ruling class or political elite get favorable treatment, while the vast majority of people get little or nothing. For example, in medieval Europe the barons and the bishops enjoyed plenty, while the common people made do with scraps and leftovers.

- By **prices**. For example, scarcity drives up price, so those who pay the top price get the scarce items. In other words, when the quantity supplied is less than the quantity demanded at the prevailing price, the price goes up. This price increase reduces the quantity demanded and increases the quantity supplied until the quantity demanded equals the quantity supplied at the new price.

Rationing by quota is inefficient because it restricts personal freedom to choose, and because it results in corruption, crime, black markets, and other ways to game the system. The result is an inefficient, unproductive economy - which played a large part in the collapse of the Soviet Union. The Soviet Union's economy proved unable to generate enough income to pay for the cost of the military spending required to keep up with the U.S. That caused the Soviet Union to fall apart and ended the "cold war." Another example is the stark difference between South and North Korea. North Korea was more affluent until the mid-1960s, but now is one of the most impoverished nations in the world. Meanwhile South Korea, under strong rule of law and property rights, is the 10th largest economy in the world. North Korea is still rationing food and basic necessities, but their situation is getting worse as time goes by. Meanwhile South Korea is projected to surpass Italy and France in terms of GDP in the near future.

Rationing by favoritism or patronage, such as crony capitalism, destroys the incentive of common people to work hard or to be creative. Why? Because whatever they produce by hard work or creativity will be appropriated and enjoyed by the ruling elite, leaving those who were productive or creative no better off than those who were unproductive and uncreative. Favoritism or patronage is usually found in nations run by dictators, or tightly controlled by the ruling elite, or that are extremely corrupt. In all these cases, the economy is extremely inefficient, and average per capita incomes are very low.

Rationing by price is efficient because it generates voluntary exchanges, which increase the wealth of all participants, and result in an efficient economy.

"Fundamentally prices serve three functions.

> 1. First, they transmit information. This function of prices is essential for enabling economic activity to be coordinated. Prices transmit information about tastes, about resource availability, about productive possibilities.

> 2. A second function that prices perform is to provide an incentive for people to adopt the least costly methods of production and to use available resources for the most highly

valued uses. They perform that function because of the third function of prices.

3. The third function of prices is to determine who gets what, and also how much they get. In other words, prices determine who earns what income. Income (also known as profit or earnings) is the difference between the cost and the selling price of items bought and sold by individual enterprises. Therefore it is prices that govern profits, and prices influence who gets what and how much under competition — in other words, the distribution of income.

The Law of Demand

People respond to price changes by adjusting their quantity purchased. This is known as the "law of demand" and it states that, on average consumers will purchase lower quantities of goods when prices go up and higher quantities of goods when prices go down. It also explains why more people buy a Toyota than a BMW or Mercedes auto, because a Toyota is less expensive than a BMW or Mercedes auto. Further, it explains why Wal-Mart and Target sell more jewelry than Tiffany's.

The "law of demand" can be illustrated by the following example:
Imagine that the demand for widgets at various prices is as follows:

---

5 Friedman, Milton. 1988. "Market Mechanisms and Central Economic Planning." In *Ideas, Their Origins, and Their Consequences* by G.Warren Nutter. Washington, DC: American Enterprise Institute for Public Policy Research: 27–46.

prices influence who gets what and how much under competition — in other words, the distribution of income.

Imagine that the demand for widgets at various prices is as follows:

<u>Table 3-1</u>

Quantity Demanded	Price per Widget
100	$14
200	$12
300	$11
400	$10
500	$9

We can plot the total cost for each quantity of units produced. The result is the Demand Curve, as shown in Chart 3-1.

<u>Chart 3-1</u>

Demand Curve

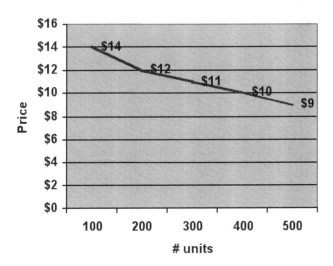

As Chart 3-1 shows, the demand curve slopes down towards the right, indicating that the quantity demanded increases as the price decreases.

Price Elasticity of Demand

Prices of goods can fluctuate. So we must ask how changes in price may affect the quantities of goods that are purchased. The percentage change in total quantity purchased divided by the percentage change in price is known as "price elasticity of demand." For example, if the price of gasoline increases by 25%, people may reduce nonessential driving, and cut their purchases of gasoline by 15%. In this case, the price elasticity of demand is 15% (percentage change in total quantity purchased) divided by 25% (percentage change in price) which is 0.6. Elasticity greater than 1 is considered elastic, and elasticity less than one is considered inelastic. Therefore elasticity of 0.6 in our gasoline example is considered inelastic.

Generally, demand that is elastic represents goods that are seen as luxuries, and that are not regarded as necessities. Therefore people will purchase much lower quantities of luxury goods if prices go up significantly. On the other hand, demand that is inelastic represents goods that are regarded as necessities. Therefore people will continue to purchase only slightly lower quantities if prices go up significantly - as in our gasoline example.

Elasticity of demand is largely determined by the availability of substitutes. The greater the availability of substitutes, the greater the price elasticity of demand. Examples are as follows:

- The price elasticity of demand for emergency medical care is low (because there are few substitutes for medical treatment of broken arms or legs);

- The price elasticity of demand for ice cream is high (because there are many substitutes for ice cream, including frozen yogurt, sherbet, and frozen soy desserts).

Elasticity of demand is not the only kind of elasticity. In addition to the elasticity of <u>demand</u> there is elasticity of <u>supply</u>. Elasticity of supply describes how suppliers of goods or services respond to a change in price. Suppliers respond to price changes by adjusting their quantity supplied. This is known as the "law of supply" and it states that, on average suppliers will supply larger quantities of goods when prices go up, and lower quantities of goods when prices go down. For example if the average price of a home increases from $200,000 to $250,000, then home builders are willing to build more homes for sale. But if the average price of a home decreases from $200,000 to $150,000, then home builders are willing to build fewer homes for sale.

Price Elasticity of Supply

The percentage change in total quantity supplied divided by the percentage change in price is known as "price elasticity of supply." For example, if the average price of a home increases by 25%, home builders become willing to increase their output of homes by

10%. In this case, the price elasticity of supply is 10% (percentage change in total quantity supplied) divided by 25% (percentage change in price) which is 0.4. Elasticity greater than 1 is considered elastic, and elasticity less than one is considered inelastic. Therefore the elasticity of supply of 0.4 in our home building example is considered inelastic.

Supply is always more elastic in the long term than in the short term, because in the long term there is time to build more production capacity.

Elasticity of demand and supply is not just an academic theory. Here is an example of elasticity of demand and supply that reflects the practicality of the real world.

Pizzeria Siciliana

Last month Pizzeria Siciliana sold 3,000 pizzas at an average price of $10 each. This month they sold 3,300 at an average price of $9 each. Calculate this month's price elasticity of demand for these pizzas. Is the demand elastic or inelastic? What does your answer mean to consumers and the supplier?

If Pizzeria Siciliana could get an average price of $11 per pizza, they would be willing to sell 3,600 pizzas. Calculate the price elasticity of supply for these pizzas. Is the supply elastic or inelastic? What does your answer mean to consumers and the supplier?

Table 3-2

Summary of Quantity and Price Information

	Demand Quantity	Demand Price	Supply Quantity	Supply Price
Last Month	3,000	$10	3,000	$10
This Month	3,300	$9	3,600	$11
Change	300	$1	600	$1
% Change	10%	10%	20%	10%
Elasticity	10%/10%	= 1.0	20%/10%	= 2.0

Elasticity equal to 1 (unit elasticity) is neither elastic nor inelastic: it is right in-between the two. Unit elasticity means that the total amount spent on the good in question remains approximately constant, despite the changes in quantity and price.

Last month Pizzeria Siciliana sold 3,000 pizzas at an average unit price of $10, for a total of 3,000 x $10 = $30,000. This month they sold 3,300 pizzas at an average unit price of $9, for a total of 3,300 x $9 = $29,700, which is not very different from $30,000.

But profit this month will be down even though they sold 300 more pizzas. Why? Because they incurred the extra cost to produce 300 more pizzas while total revenue did not increase. Assume that it costs $6 to make each pizza.

Table 3-3

Effect on Profit

	Last Month	This Month
Sales	3,000 x $10	3,300 x $9
Total Sales	$30,000	$29,700
Costs at $6 each	$18,000	$19,800
Profit	$12,000	$9,900

The moral: suppliers faced with unit elasticity of demand have little incentive to increase output and sales. Increased output and sales will raise costs but not revenues, and the result is reduced profits.

The next scenario involves Pizzeria Siciliana increasing price to $11 per pizza and wanting to sell 3,600 pizzas. Elasticity of supply would be (% change in quantity)/(% change in price) = (600/3,000)/($1/$10) = (0.2/0.1) = 2.0 = elasticity > 1 = elastic supply. It is important to note that this is elasticity of *supply*, not elasticity of *demand*. Just because Pizzeria Siciliana is willing to supply 3,600 pizzas at a price of $11, does not mean that consumers would buy 3,600 pizzas at a price of $11.

What does this price increase mean to consumers? With a price increase of $1 per pizza, consumers will buy <u>fewer</u> pizzas. At unit elasticity they will buy about $30,000/$11 = about 2,727 pizzas, rather than 3,000. So Pizzeria Siciliana is dreaming if they think they can up the price by $1 and sell more pizzas.

But, even if Pizzeria Siciliana cannot sell more pizzas at $11, the price increase will still raise profits. Now they can obtain total revenue of about $30,000 by producing only 2,727 pizzas – which will lower their costs. So this would be a profitable move for Pizzeria Siciliana to make.

Table 3-4

Effect on Profit

	<u>Last Month</u>	<u>This Month</u>
Sales Units & Price	3,000 x $10	2,727 x $11
Sales Dollars	$30,000	$29,997
Costs at $6 each	$18,000	$16,362
Income (Profit)	$12,000	$13,635

<u>The moral</u>: suppliers faced with unit elasticity of demand have an incentive to increase price and to accept the resulting lower output and sales. With unit elasticity of demand, lower output and sales will reduce costs but will not reduce revenues, which will in turn raise profits.

Importance of Elasticity in the Real World

Finally, it pays to know the price elasticity of demand in your business. Elasticity is not just some obscure economic theory: it is valuable practical information. Many businesses use market segmentation to sell at lower prices to customers with very elastic demand, while getting higher prices from customers with inelastic demand. Here are a few familiar examples:

- Senior discounts and student discounts at movies, restaurants, theme parks, and stores.
- Ladies' nights and "happy hours" at bars.
- "Early Bird" discounted prices for early diners at restaurants.
- Standby airfares on commercial airlines.
- Supermarket coupons.
- Discounts for students, teachers and professors on computers, computer supplies and software.

The consumers receiving the discounts are those with the highest price elasticity. It follows that the higher the price elasticity of demand of the average customer, the more the supplier will need to accept lower prices. What it boils down to is that price elasticity of demand puts limits on the market power of suppliers. The greater the price elasticity of demand, the lower the market power of suppliers.

Remember that price elasticity of demand depends largely on the availability of substitutes. So it makes sense that the greater the availability of substitutes, the less market power the suppliers of the particular good or service will have. The greater the availability of substitutes, the more that suppliers become price takers, rather than price makers.

Chapter Summary

- Effective demand means the quantity is actually purchased, not just what consumers might desire.
- Demand varies with price. The Law of Demand states: the lower the price, the greater the quantity demanded.
- Scarcity means that there must be rationing of goods and services.
- Rationing can be done by:
    - Physical quotas: x pairs of shoes per year.
    - Favoritism or patronage: only the nobility are allowed to hunt deer or eat venison.
    - Prices: whoever has the money can buy the goods.
- Rationing by quota is inefficient because it restricts personal freedom to choose, and it results in corruption, crime, black markets, and other ways to game the system.
- Rationing by favoritism or patronage destroys the incentive of common people to work hard or to be creative, because whatever they produce by hard work or creativity will be confiscated and enjoyed by the ruling elite
- Rationing by price is efficient because it generates voluntary exchanges, which increase the wealth of all participants, and result in an efficient economy.
- The price elasticity of demand states how the quantity demanded changes in relation to price.
- Price elasticity of demand depends largely on the availability of substitutes.
- Price elasticity of demand is used in business to charge higher prices to customers with inelastic demand and lower prices to customers with elastic demand.
- The availability of substitutes determines the degree of market power wielded by suppliers.

Discussion Questions

1. In the vast majority of cases, the lower the price, the greater the quantity demanded. But in rare instances, this law of demand has exceptions. For example, if the price of food goes up, people may buy more bread, because bread is cheaper than most foods, and so people buy more of the cheapest food and much less of the expensive foods. Goods of this type are called "inferior goods." How many inferior goods in addition to bread can you think of?

2. Which of the following goods and services have elastic demand:

   - Domino's pizza?
   - Colgate toothpaste?
   - McDonald's hamburgers?
   - Heart transplants?
   - Appearances on the American Idol TV Show?
   - Caviar?
   - Apple computers?
   - Microsoft Office?
   - Dom Perignon champagne?

3. Why are standby airfares cheaper than regular economy fares? And why are fares with Saturday stopovers cheaper than weekday fares?

4. Health care is rationed in the U.S. by various means. Health care may be accessed through:

   a. Medicare (for seniors),
   b. Medicaid (for people unable to afford health care),
   c. Health Maintenance Organizations (HMO's) where patients pay a fixed annual fee and then get treated

only by those physicians who are authorized members of the HMO,

    d. Preferred Provider Organizations (PPO's) which are similar to HMO's, but which also allow patients to get treatment, at extra fees, from physicians who are not authorized members of the PPO.

    e. Open health insurance, where patients can get treatment from any physician of their choice.

Which of these means of delivering health care represent rationing by:

    i.   Physical quotas;
    ii. Favoritism or patronage;
    iii. Prices:
    iv. A combination of the above methods?

5. How much market power does each of the following have:

- Your local supermarket?
- Your local gas station?
- Your local dry cleaner?
- Your electric company?
- Your phone company?
- Your post office?
- Your cable TV provider?
- Your dentist?
- Your health insurance carrier?

6. How does the availability of substitutes affect whether a supplier is a price maker or a price taker?

Chapter 4: The Supply of Goods and Services

I am like any other man. All I do is supply a demand.

Al Capone

What is Cost?

Cost is a sacrifice of resources. For example, when a business purchases inventory for resale, it pays out cash in order to purchase the goods. The sacrifice is the cash paid out, in order to obtain the inventory. This sacrifice is known as an explicit cost, and is also called an "out of pocket" cost.

In addition to explicit costs, there are implicit costs, which are also known as "opportunity costs." Opportunity cost is the value of the opportunity that was sacrificed in order to take the opportunity that was accepted. When a high-priced consultant travels to Europe by ship instead of flying, the opportunity cost of the ocean cruise is the fees that could have been earned in the extra time it took to go by sea rather than by air.

Decision-making involves making choices. All choices concern the future: so past or "sunk" costs are irrelevant for decision-making. For example, you are considering trading-in your auto for a newer model. What you initially paid for your auto is irrelevant because it relates to the past, which cannot be changed. It is a "sunk cost." The only costs relevant to this decision are the cost of the new car and the allowance the dealer will give you for your old car.

Relevant costs are incremental or marginal costs, which are the additional costs caused by the decision under consideration. For example, say you are planning to drive to Dallas, TX from your office in Columbus, OH. A colleague asks if she can ride with you from Columbus to Dallas. What is the incremental or marginal cost of taking her along? Since you will be going anyway, the only incremental or marginal cost of her riding along is the additional gasoline used by your auto due to her added weight.

Marginal and Average Costs

It is important to distinguish between marginal and average costs. Here is an example to clarify marginal and average costs. Imagine that a widget factory can produce various amounts of widgets at the following costs:

Table 4-1

Quantity Produced	Total Cost	Incremental Total Cost	Marginal Cost per Unit	Average Cost per Unit
100	$1,000		$10 ($1,000/100)	$10 ($1,000/100)
200	$2,200	$1,200	$12 ($1,200/100)	$11 ($2,200/200)
300	$3,600	$1,400	$14 ($1,400/100)	$12 ($3,600/300)
400	$5,200	$1,600	$16 ($1,600/100)	$13 ($5,200/400)
500	$7,000	$1,800	$18 ($1,800/100)	$14 ($7,000/500)

Notice that marginal cost per unit is the cost of the last unit produced. Average cost per unit is total cost divided by total number of units produced – which is a cumulative number, as opposed to marginal cost per unit, which is an incremental number, rather than a cumulative number.

We can plot the total cost for each quantity of units produced. The result is the Supply Curve, as shown in Chart 4-1.

Chart 4-1

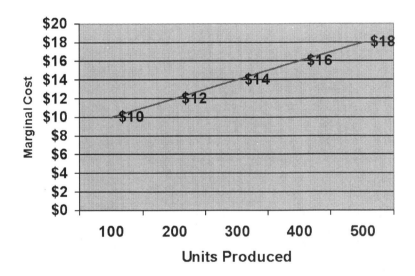

As Chart 4-1 shows, with each increase in price, suppliers are willing to sell more units. This is known as the Law of Supply. Supply curves slope upwards to the right – as opposed to demand curves, which slope downwards to the right. In a later chapter we will explore how demand and supply curves interact with one another. But for now, we need to discuss the elasticity of supply.

44

Price Elasticity of Supply

Price elasticity of supply is the percentage change in the quantity supplied divided by the percentage change in the price. If this ratio is > 1, supply is elastic. If this ratio is < 1, supply is inelastic. Supply is always more elastic in the long term than in the short term, because in the long term there is time to build more production capacity.

The distinction between long term and short term is very important. Say that the supplier is currently producing and selling 300 units at a total cost of $3,600, which Table 4-1 shows is an average unit cost of $12. They are selling these units at $18 each, for total revenue of $5,400, and a total profit of $1,800 (which is total revenue of $5,400 less total cost of $3,600).

Now assume that this supplier gets an offer from a customer to purchase 100 units at $17 each. Should this offer be accepted?

If it is accepted, total revenue will increase by 100 units at $17 = $1,700, which will raise total revenue from $5,400 to $7,100 for 400 units. Total cost for 400 units in Table 4-1 is $5,200. Therefore total profit becomes total revenue of $7,100 less total cost of $5,200 = $1,900. At 300 units of output, total profit was $1,800. So acceptance of the new order would increase profit from $1,800 to $1,900 which is an increase of $100.

This increased profit of $100 suggests that the supplier should accept the new order. Is that our final answer? No: there is a catch.

The catch

What if our existing customers find out that we are selling units at $17, while they are paying $18 per unit? It is a reliable prediction that our existing customers will also demand to pay $17 per unit. In that case, we will still sell 400 units, now at $17 each, for total revenue of $6,800. But total cost still remains at $5,200 for 400 units. Therefore profit will now be $1,600 (total revenue of $6,800 less total cost of $5,200). But total profit was $1,800 when only 300 units were being sold. So, under this condition, the new order should be declined.

What is the lesson here? It was profitable to accept the new order at a price below usual, provided that existing customers either could not find out about the cut price, or provided that existing customers could not reasonably expect to pay the lower price. How could that be accomplished?

<u>Market Segmentation</u>

It is accomplished by market segmentation, where one customer segment cannot expect to pay the same price as another segment. This is the case where segments are created by differences in gender, in age, or in other characteristics that cannot be hidden or switched. Here are examples of those types of segmentation, which you will probably recall, because we have presented before, in Chapter 3:

- Senior discounts and student discounts at movies, restaurants, theme parks, stores.

- Ladies' nights and "happy hours" at bars.

- "Early Bird" discounted prices for early diners at restaurants.
  - Standby airfares on commercial airlines.
  - Discounts for students, teachers and professors on computer software

In each of the above cases, the discounted prices could be restricted to those customers who belonged to the discount segment. For seniors and students, ID could be verified from driver licenses and student ID cards. Similarly, ladies' night discounts could be restricted to females, "happy hours" and "early birds" are restricted by the time of day, and discounts for teachers and professors can be restricted to those who can show paycheck stubs (with dollar amounts blacked out).

These segments were based on price elasticity of demand. Customer segments with inelastic demand are charged higher prices, and customers with elastic demand pay lower prices. Price elasticity of demand depends heavily on the availability of substitutes. So customer segments with inelastic demand are those who lack readily available substitutes for the good in question. Conversely, customer segments with elastic demand are those who have readily available substitutes for the good in question.

Therefore businesses tend to restrict discounts to customers who can be verified as members of specific market segments. Customers who are not members of those segments can be charged full price, based on their less elastic demand.

Chapter Summary

- Cost is a sacrifice of resources, usually made in order to obtain a more highly valued good or service.
- Explicit costs are actual payments made, and implicit costs are sacrifices of other opportunities, known as opportunity costs.
- Relevant costs are those costs affected by any particular choice. Therefore relevant costs are incremental or marginal costs, which are the additional costs caused by the decision under consideration.
- Sunk costs are never relevant, and are costs already incurred, and therefore not affected by the decision under consideration.
- Supply curves are plots of supply quantities against the total cost of each quantity supplied.
- The Law of Supply states that the quantity supplied will increase as the price increases – as opposed to the Law of Demand, which states that the quantity demanded will decrease as the price increases.
- Suppliers will sell at higher prices to customer segments with inelastic demand, and at lower prices to customer segments with elastic demand.

Discussion Questions

1. A large corporation is considering building an auto plant in India. In order to finance the construction of the new plant in India, the corporation will borrow the needed funds from a bank. Since the plant will be built with the bank's money, will it be free of cost to the corporation? If so, why? If not, what sacrifice represents the cost of the plant to the corporation?

2. Ajax Corporation has the option to acquire Beejax

Corporation for $800 million, or to repay its existing $800 million debt owed to the bank, thereby saving interest payments of $80 million per year. What is the explicit cost of acquiring Beejax Corporation? What is the implicit opportunity cost of acquiring Beejax Corporation?

3. Ajax Corporation previously owned 10% of Beejax Corporation, for which it had paid $3 million 7 years ago. The $800 million is the additional cost to acquire the remaining 90% of Beejax Corporation. Therefore the total cost to Ajax Corporation of its 100% interest in Beejax Corporation is $803 million. How much is the incremental cost of acquiring Beejax Corporation? How much is the Ajax Corporation sunk cost relating to Beejax Corporation?

4. Beach Manufacturing Company sells building materials to construction companies, to building owners, to repairmen, and to do-it-yourselfers. Can each of these be treated as separate customer segments? If so, how can Beach Manufacturing Company restrict discounted prices to members of each particular customer segment? Which segments will pay higher prices and which segments will pay lower prices, and why?

5. Most airlines have frequent flyer plans. Why do they have these frequent flyer plans, and how, if at all, might these plans relate to customer elasticity of demand?

6. What is the difference between sunk costs and incremental costs? Before they were incurred, were sunk costs actually incremental costs?

Chapter 5: Supply and Demand

Deliberation, n.: The act of examining one's bread to determine which side it is buttered on.

Ambrose Bierce

The Market

The market is where suppliers and buyers interact to transact exchanges of goods and services. Up to this point we have referred to a market or to markets, without defining what we mean by those terms. In economics, a market is any kind of arrangement where buyers and sellers can make exchanges. It may be a supermarket, or a department store, or a trading floor in a stock exchange or commodity exchange. It may be a physical place, or it may be over the telephone, or online, or by mail, or even by secret signals at auction houses like Sotheby's. What we mean by a market is very broad. All that is required is that buyers and sellers can communicate in order to trade.

Markets are complex processes of bids and offers, sometimes made more efficient by organizations, such as middlemen, designed to reduce transaction costs and thus facilitate exchanges. For example, say that you want to purchase a certain book. Most books are produced by a chain of organizations, starting with an author, who submits a manuscript to a literary agent, who sells it to a publisher, who contracts it out first to a proofreader/editor, then to a printer, and subsequently to a book wholesaler, who sells it to a retail bookstore, where you can buy it. In-between you, the consumer, and the author, stand several middlemen, namely the literary agent, the publisher, the proofreader/editor, the printer, the book wholesaler, and the book retailer. Why are all these middlemen necessary?

Middlemen in the Publishing Industry

Publishers are flooded with manuscripts from budding authors, and most publishers refuse to accept any manuscripts "over the transom." They will only review manuscripts submitted by literary agents, because these agents know how to distinguish a viable commercial manuscript from a dud that will not sell, and these agents also know what type of manuscripts each publisher is interested in. For example, some publishers only publish fiction, some only publish non-fiction, some specialize in children's' books or teen books or textbooks or cookbooks or religious books or paperbacks, or romances. So literary agents perform the useful function of channeling manuscripts to their most likely targets (often the wastebasket).

A well-known story tells about the author who became impatient about the long time that a publisher was taking in responding to his manuscript. The author wrote the publisher a letter, saying "Kindly let me know immediately if you are accepting or rejecting my manuscript. I need to know now, because if you reject it I have other irons in the fire." The publisher replied: "We suggest that you put your manuscript with your other irons."

Publishers have limited resources to spend on producing books, and often have little or no way to reliably predict how well any book may sell. Therefore they tend to publish books that appear more likely to sell because they have been written by well-known authors with a track record for producing best-sellers. So one function of a publisher is to weed out potential books that seem unlikely to achieve commercial success, and to focus on potential winners. Naturally, they blunder from time to time and turn down some excellent books, and accept some real duds. But, mostly, they provide an efficient filter that accepts books likely to be in demand, and rejects books that are unlikely to be in demand.

Proofreader/editors are like the plasterers and painters who transform the bare walls and ugly cement of unfinished houses into desirable dwellings. They turn ugly into handsome. Proofreaders/editors turn clumsy phrases into graceful prose and typos into correct language. By so doing, they add value to the book.

Book wholesalers serve the market as distribution channels, enabling all copies of the book to leave one central location and to be delivered to each region of the country or even the world. From their regional warehouses, these wholesalers break bulk and dispatch smaller quantities of the book to individual retail bookstores. In some cases, the book wholesalers also provide storage and credit terms to individual retail bookstores. In those ways, the book wholesalers add value to the book.

Finally the book retailer makes the book available to the end user at convenient locations, and often in pleasant surroundings, which are sometimes enhanced with armchairs, coffee bars, and background music.

The key point is that middlemen provide useful services, which consumers are willing to pay for. Middlemen are not parasites, as is sometimes inaccurately said, but play a useful and efficient role in getting the desired good or service to its final consumer. Of course, one can sometimes eliminate a middleman, but one cannot eliminate his or her function. For example, an author can cut out literary agents and publishers by self-publishing a manuscript. But then that author will need to edit and proofread the manuscript, find a printer, and promote, distribute and market the book. So the self-publishing author has not eliminated the middleman, but merely replicated the middleman function.

Automatic Market Adjustment Through The Price Mechanism

Free markets are self-adjusting through price changes. If more is demanded than is supplied, the price automatically increases to call forth more supply and to reduce demand. If less is demanded than is supplied, the price falls to supply and increase demand.

This automatic process of adjustment clears the markets by balancing supply with demand through the price mechanism. Prices are signals that coordinate supply with demand. We can illustrate this by recalling our previous discussions of the demand curve, and the supply curve, and putting both of them together.

Table 5-1

Quantity Demanded	Price per Widget
100	$14
200	$12
300	$11
400	$10
500	$9

Table 5-2

Quantity Produced	Total Cost	Incremental Total Cost	Marginal Cost per Unit	Average Cost per Unit
100	$1,000		$10 ($1,000/100)	$10 ($1,000/100)
200	$2,200	$1,200	$12 ($1,200/100)	$11 ($2,200/200)
300	$3,600	$1,400	$14 ($1,400/100)	$12 ($3,600/300)
400	$5,200	$1,600	$16 ($1,600/100)	$13 ($5,200/400)
500	$7,000	$1,800	$18 ($1,800/100)	$14 ($7,000/500)

Chart 5-1

Demand & Supply

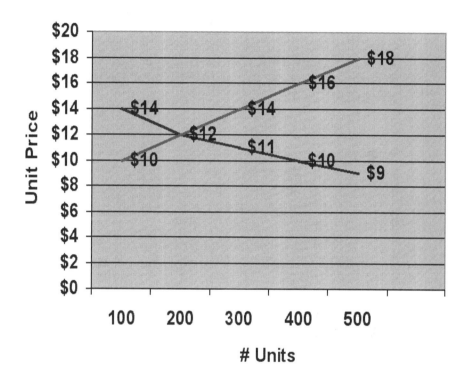

As Chart 5-1 shows, the blue demand curve and the red supply curve cross at 200 units and a unit price of $12. That means that a price of $12 is where the quantity demanded equals the quantity supplied. At the $12 price the market will clear. In other words, supply and demand have been balanced through the price system.

If the price was $10, the quantity demanded would have been 400 units, but only 100 units would have been supplied, resulting in a shortage of 300 units. That shortage would cause the price to rise, which would simultaneously raise the quantity supplied and reduce the quantity demanded, so that the shortage would be eliminated and the market would clear

By the same token, if the price was $16, the quantity demanded would have been zero units, but 400 units would have been supplied, resulting in a surplus of 400 units. That surplus would cause the price to fall, which would simultaneously lower the quantity supplied and increase the quantity demanded, so that the surplus would be eliminated and the market would clear.

Free markets are self-adjusting through the price mechanism. If more is demanded than is supplied, the price automatically increases to call forth more supply and to reduce demand. If less is demanded than is supplied, the price falls to reduce supply and increase demand.

This automatic price mechanism clears markets by balancing supply with demand. Prices are signals that coordinate supply with demand.

When a society interferes with these price signals, by curtailing free markets in favor of centralized planning, price signals are lost. Then supply and demand become uncoordinated and the results are shortages and surpluses.

Externalities

Up to now we have implicitly assumed that all of the cost of a good is incurred by its supplier. For example, if I buy stainless steel cutlery from a supplier, we assume that the supplier paid all the costs of producing that stainless steel cutlery. But what if the steel mill that produced the steel for the cutlery polluted the air with sulphuric acid that caused acid rain, and polluted the water table with chemicals used in the process. The pollution harms people in the area who breathe the air, while acid rain damages nearby agricultural crops, and chemicals in the water table seep into neighborhood wells used for drinking water, causing cancer in local residents. The cost of the pollution falls on people in the area who suffer illness, premature death and expensive medical treatment.

These unfortunate people in the area bear part of the cost of producing the steel, and the steel mill escapes paying for those costs that are inherent in making steel. Economists call this an "externality" because part of the cost of making the steel is paid by parties external to the steel mill. This externality has several negative effects, as follows:

- As stated, it imposes harmful and unwanted costs on people who are neither suppliers nor consumers of the stainless steel cutlery. These costs are forced on these unfortunate people against their will, and contrary to their best interests.
- The externality reduces economic efficiency, because it is not a voluntary free market transaction that produces wealth. In fact, it reduces the wealth of the unfortunate people harmed by the pollution.
- By the steel mill escaping part of the inherent cost of their product, they in fact receive a subsidy. As we learned earlier, subsidies result in surpluses. Therefore more steel is produced than is justified by the operation of the price mechanism in free markets, which reduces economic efficiency and wealth.

Externalities can be negative, as in the example we have just discussed, and in many more forms such as reckless or drunk driving, criminal behavior, spreading infections and illness, being violent, noisy or rude, or even littering. Or externalities can be positive. For example, say that my next door neighbor is fond of gardening, and that I benefit by sharing the delightful aroma of her roses and her honeysuckle, as well as receiving shade from her oak tree, and apples from branches of her apple tree that overhang my yard. She also generously gives me surplus strawberries and tomatoes from her garden. And to top it off, the beautifully landscaped grounds of her house enhance the appearance of the neighborhood, and add to the resale value of nearby homes.

Although there are positive externalities, economics mostly focuses on finding solutions for the problems caused by negative externalities. One solution is passing laws that ban pollution and other negative externalities, and impose penalties on violators. A more flexible solution is to impose a tax on negative externalities such as pollution, because then polluters would be able to devise their own solutions to cut pollution, or, alternatively, continue to pollute and to pay the tax – which then internalizes the externality, so that the polluter no longer imposes costs on others, but rather bears the cost of polluting, instead of evading this cost. In the interest of economic efficiency, it is generally best to avoid imposing arbitrary "one size fits all" coercive solutions like laws that ban pollution and other negative externalities, and impose penalties on violators. A more flexible approach, such as a tax on pollution, is preferable in order to internalize the externality, and thereby to restore the functioning of the price mechanism.

Chapter Summary

- A market is any arrangement where buyers and sellers can makes exchanges.

- Middlemen are important participants in markets, because they serve several purposes, such as facilitating contacts between buyers and sellers, and reducing transaction costs.

- Middlemen are not parasites. They can be eliminated, but their functions can never be eliminated.

- Free markets are automatically self-adjusting and self-clearing through operation of the price mechanism.

- When a society interferes with these price signals, by curtailing free markets in favor of centralized planning, price signals are lost. Then supply and demand become uncoordinated and the results are shortages and surpluses.

- Externalities interfere with price signals and reduce efficiency. It is best to avoid imposing coercive solutions like laws that ban pollution and other negative externalities. A more flexible approach, such as a tax on pollution, is preferable in order to internalize the externality, and thereby to restore the functioning of the price mechanism

Discussion Questions

1. Which of the following are markets?

   - Your local supermarket?

- Wal-Mart?

- Starbucks?

- Your local gas station?

- Your local public school?

- Your local public library?

- A private country club?

- City hall?

- A newspaper?

2. Which of the following are middlemen, and why?

- A wholesaler?

- Your local drugstore or pharmacy?

- Your dentist?

- Your bank?

- NBC News?

- The United Nations?

- The British Parliament?

- The PGA Tour?

- Microsoft Corporation?

3. My spouse just cannot stand bargaining with an auto dealer. So I buy the cars whenever we need a new one. Now I have become a middleman, and the supply chain between the auto manufacturer and my spouse has become longer. Is this economically efficient? Why or why not?

4. How efficient are the economies of North Korea and Cuba, compared With Canada? Why are the North Korean and Cuban economies more efficient or less efficient that the Canadian economy?

5. The U.S. government subsidizes ethanol and other bio-fuels. Does this make the U.S. economy more efficient or less efficient? Why?

6. I halt my auto at a red light. A car pulls up next to me with bald tires, an exhaust pipe belching black smoke, and a stereo blaring loud rap sounds. Are these positive or negative externalities, and why?

Chapter 6: Supply and Demand Issues

I always say don't make plans, make options.

Jennifer Aniston

Price controls are imposed by government, usually as a result of political pressure. Typically, price controls are well-intended. But price controls prevent the price mechanism from operating properly so that markets clear. Therefore price controls inevitably cause shortages or surpluses. Price controls are normally well-intended, but they often have unexpected consequences.

Price controls come in two varieties. Some price controls are price ceilings that set an upper limit on prices that can be charged. Other price controls are price floors that set a fixed minimum on prices that can be charged. An example of a price ceiling is rent control, which sets an upper limit to the rent that landlords can charge tenants. Price ceilings tend to cause shortages, because prices cannot rise when shortages occur, in order to call forth greater supply to alleviate the shortage. Rent control has been imposed in New York City and in Santa Monica, CA. In both cases the result was that landlords cut back on maintenance of rental buildings, and ceased to build more rental units.

That resulted in shortages of available rental space. As a result, people in rent-controlled buildings became unwilling to move out, because they could not find alternative accommodations, and that aggravated the shortages of rental units. If renters were forced to move, because of death or ill-health or other compelling reasons, they demanded illicit under-the-table "key money" from new tenants, which created black markets in rental units. So corruption crept into the rental market, making it yet less competitive by further damaging the price mechanism.

Another price ceiling is anti-gouging laws which prohibit vendors from raising prices after natural disasters such as hurricanes in the eastern and southern coastal regions of the U.S. At first anti-gouging laws seem like a helpful regulation designed to protect people harmed by storm damage from unscrupulous profiteers, who are intent on fleecing the victims of the storm. But experience has taught storm victims that these well-intended regulations actually make a bad situation worse, and cause harm to the very people that they were designed to protect.

For example, after hurricanes in the South destroyed houses and blew off roofs, there were lengthy shortages of building materials needed for reconstruction. If prices had been allowed to rise, supplies of building materials would have poured into the South, attracted by the higher prices, and the shortages would have soon been eliminated. Very soon, with excess supply, prices would then fall back down to more customary levels. People displaced from their homes could have speedily repaired and rebuilt, and moved back home. But the anti-gouging laws caused shortages of building materials that often lasted a long time, and that greatly slowed recovery from the disaster. Price ceilings often cause shortages, and always harm the very people that they are intended to help.

Price floors also are well-intended, but inherently harmful. One example of a price floor is the minimum wage. Setting a minimum wage is intended to protect unskilled workers by providing them with a "living wage." That is the visible idea. But what actually happens is that employers of unskilled workers find that the increase in the minimum wage now makes it more expensive to hire unskilled workers. So employers cut back on hiring, fire less productive employees who are no longer worth their increased pay, and search out substitutes for unskilled labor, such as outsourcing jobs to developing countries where labor is less expensive, or hiring illegal immigrants, or purchasing machines that can do the work more cheaply.

As a result, the lowest-skilled workers lose their jobs, and go from low pay to no pay. The very lowest-skilled workers that the minimum wage was supposed to help end up unemployed and unemployable. In some countries where the minimum wage is relatively high, such as France, youth unemployment is as high as 40%, and there are no baggers in the supermarkets. In turn, the French have to bag and carry out their own groceries because the high minimum wage has rendered baggers unemployable and unaffordable.

Another form of price floor is agricultural price supports. Farmers are subsidized to grow certain crops. These subsidies on top of market prices cause farmers to increase their crop production, resulting in agricultural surpluses. These agricultural surpluses cannot be sold, and are left to rot in government storage, or burned, or otherwise inefficiently wasted.

Price floors often cause surpluses, of unskilled labor, of agricultural commodities, or whatever goods or services they are applied to. They throw sand into the smooth functioning of the price mechanism, and result in economic inefficiency and waste, as well as harming the very people they were intended to help.

Price controls, whether they are ceilings or price floors, are restrictions on free choice. They interfere with voluntary exchanges and tend to create shortages or surpluses or lead to black markets, underground activities, and criminal behavior. Free market prices lead to coordinated supply and demand, so that markets clear and the economy is efficient.

The Politics of Wage Controls

Earlier we wrote that economics and politics are completely different from each other.

1. Economics is based upon logic and upon factual evidence. That is how we know that larger quantities of a good or a service are likely to be purchased at lower prices than at higher prices. And that is how economic principles are derived – everything is based on logic and on factual evidence. Economics is all about efficiency. It can analyze choices that

tell us what alternative is most efficient. There are right and wrong answers in economics - so far as economic efficiency is concerned.

2. In contrast, politics is not based on logic or on factual evidence. Rather, politics is based on values. Values are not a matter of logic or factual evidence, but instead are personal preferences. There are no right and wrong answers in politics, only different values. So no value can be better or worse than any other value. In politics, values matter much more than economic efficiency. These values may be things like patriotism, or environmentalism, or animal rights, or same-sex marriage, or egalitarianism, or collective versus individual decision-making.

So economics and politics are different and distinct from each other. Please bear in mind that this book deals only with economics, and never with politics. Nothing here is about Democrat or Republican. In that case, how do we explain why Democrats tend to support price controls, while Republicans tend to oppose price controls?

With respect to price ceilings, like rent control, I suspect that most politicians (both Democrat and Republican) are not familiar with economics, and may not understand the economic implications of price ceilings. The same is probably true about anti-price-gouging laws. However, politicians are keenly interested in being elected or re-elected, and anti-price-gouging laws are generally popular. So their desire to be elected or re-elected probably goes a long way to explain why politicians support anti-price-gouging laws. As the scriptures say, "forgive them, for they know not what they do."

But with respect to price floors, like the minimum wage, it may be a different story. Even though politicians (both Democrat and Republican) are not familiar with economics, it is fairly widely recognized that the minimum wage can cause unemployment among the most unskilled workers. Therefore even politicians tend to be restrained when setting the minimum wage. Rather than setting the minimum wage at a high level (say $100 per hour), minimum wages tend to be set at a more modest level (such as $8 per hour), where they affect only a small minority of workers, and thus cause only minimum harm. Last, but not least, unions tend to like minimum wage laws (because they restrict competition to unionized workers from unskilled non-union workers). Since both parties vie for union campaign contributions and union votes, minimum wage laws may be favored for political purposes, despite the economic harm that minimum wage laws may cause.

Subsidies and Taxes

In addition to price controls there are other forms of government intervention in markets, including subsidies and taxes (such as sales taxes, excise taxes and customs duties). Subsidies tend to create surpluses, because when some good or service is subsidized more of it is supplied. An examples is the subsidy for ethanol (which would not be competitive without its subsidy) resulting in greater supply of ethanol than is sufficient. Note that this subsidy does not really make ethanol any cheaper. Ethanol users are enabled to buy ethanol at a lower price because of the subsidy. But the subsidy is funded out of taxes. So the lower prices for ethanol users are balanced by higher taxes paid by taxpayers.

The ethanol subsidy has an unfortunate side-effect. Ethanol is made from corn, so the greater supply of ethanol has raised the demand for corn, and corn has increased in price. Since cattle and chickens are mainly corn- fed, the increased price of corn has raised the prices of beef and chicken. In short, subsidies not only create surpluses of the subsidized good, but they can also have unintended consequences, such as causing shortages of other goods.

Taxes on goods or services increase the price of those goods or services, and tend to cause shortages. Just as subsidies cause surpluses, taxes tend to cause shortages because when anything is taxed it is made more expensive, and so we get less of it. In short, subsidies and taxes, like price controls, interfere with the price mechanism, cause surpluses or shortages, so that markets no longer clear automatically, and make the economy less efficient.

When resources are not privately owned, they are not priced by the free market and so tend to be inefficiently allocated. Here is an example of the harm that can occur when resources are not privately owned. This example has become famous, and is known as the "tragedy of the commons"[6].

The tragedy of the commons comes about as follows. Imagine a pasture open to use by all. With open access, each herder will try to feed as many cattle as possible on the commons, because the pasture is a free good. This kind of arrangement may work more or less satisfactorily so long as wars, disease and poaching hold down the numbers of humans and beasts below the carrying capacity of the pasture. Eventually, however, the day of reckoning may arrive, when wars, disease and poaching can no longer hold down the numbers of humans and beasts, and overcrowding becomes a reality. At this point, the limited carrying capacity of the commons relentlessly results in tragedy.

As a rational being, each herder acts in their own self-interest. More or less consciously, they ask, "What is the harm to me if I add one more animal to my herd?" Since use of the pasture is free to each herder, they have no hesitation in adding more and more animals to graze on the pasture. Therefore each herder keeps adding cattle to the commons, until overcrowding turns the once-fertile pasture into a bare and barren wasteland. Then all herds and their herders face starvation. When access is free to everyone, no-one limits the use of the scarce resource, and everyone becomes ruined.

---

6 Hardin, G. (1968) <u>The Tragedy of the Commons</u>, *Science* 162, 1243-1248.
 Commons are resources that are publicly owned and open to use by the public, such as public grazing lands, lakes and rivers, and sea coast.

This same problem afflicts other shared resources. For example, lakes, rivers and oceans become fished out because of excessive catches that wipe out most of the fish. In similar fashion, wild animals may eat and trample the crops of farmers, so that the farmers turn to hunting and killing these wild animals. After the animals are wiped out, tourists stop coming on safari to see the wild life, and the farmers find that the demand for their crops has dried up because the tourist business is dead.

How can this problem of "the tragedy of the commons" be avoided or solved? It has been successfully solved by converting the commons into private property. For example, if the commons was put out to auction, and the winning bidder could now charge grazing fees to users, then there would be no more "free good." The private owner would not allow the property to become over-grazed, and herders would limit their use to what they could afford to pay. This solution has been successfully used in Africa, where the ownership of wild animals has been awarded to village chiefs. In order to stimulate safari tours, the chiefs hire villagers to protect the animals from poachers, and to keep the animals out of the farmers' fields. As a result, the animals are kept in the wild, the farmers sell their crops, and tourism flourishes, bringing money to the villages.

The lesson:

1. When property is owned by everyone, it is cared for by no-one. Public ownership is not economically efficient, and can lead to "the tragedy of the commons." But with private ownership and secure property rights, property is efficiently used, to everyone's benefit.

2. When access to a resource is free, that resource will be overused. In a world of scarcity, nothing is really free. As economists like to say: "there is no such thing as a free lunch."

Let's take a closer look at what economics is all about. Economics is all about exchange. Think about every choice we make as an economic transaction. Every economic transaction involves an exchange in which we must give up something that we have in order to get something that we want. What we give up and what we receive both have value to us. A fundamental premise in economics is that the value of what we receive in a transaction is more than the value of what we give up. If what we received didn't have more value to us, we wouldn't make the exchange. By definition, we are better off after an exchange than we were before the exchange. To summarize:

- We make exchanges because (a) we tend to specialize, and are not self-sufficient, and (b) there are things we want more than the things we have;

- Other people will trade with us because there are things they want more than the things they have;

- The fact that each of us places a different value upon the same item leads to exchanges;

- Each party to a free exchange gains something – otherwise they would not participate in the exchange;

- It follows that free exchanges create wealth;

- In fact, the countries where markets are most free are the countries that are most wealthy.

Free exchanges take place in the private sector. All transactions in the private sector are voluntary, and are wealth-producing. But transactions with government are not voluntary. For example:

- Payment of income taxes is compulsory, not voluntary. If one does not pay, there will be penalties or even a jail sentence.

- No-one can drive a motor-cycle, car or truck without a driver's license and vehicle registration.

- Social security taxes are deducted from our paychecks whether or not we agree.

- If we are caught speeding we are fined.

In brief, all transactions with government are involuntary. They are forced, and are not free choices. We know that free choices are wealth-producing, because people would not freely make those choices unless all parties gained more wealth from those choices. Since transactions with government are not free choices, willingly entered into, it is impossible to say if they are wealth-producing or not.

This leads to the key question: which activities are best performed in the private sector as voluntary free choices, and which activities are best performed by government? There are various answers to this question: communists and socialists maintain that all activities should be in the public sector. Communists and socialists maintain that private property should be eliminated, and that all property should be owned by the state, which abolishes the private sector, and puts everything in the public sector. That makes communist and socialist nations fully vulnerable to "the tragedy of the commons." We see ample evidence of this vulnerability in communist and socialist nations: their infrastructures such as highways, bridges and buildings are usually in poor condition, run-down and neglected, and their economies are usually in a shambles, as we see in Cuba, Belarus, and North Korea.

Most European countries have mixed economies, combining a large public sector with a large private sector. These countries are more prosperous than communist and socialist nations, but have lower rates of economic growth and lower per capita incomes than the U.S. The U.S. has a relatively smaller public sector, and a relatively larger private sector than European nations. We also enjoy greater prosperity and higher economic growth than Europe.

Libertarians maintain that the U.S. would enjoy yet higher prosperity and growth if the public sector was substantially cut back. Essentially, libertarians argue that government should perform only the activities that cannot be performed in the private sector[3]. These activities are:

- Maintaining the military, to protect us from hostile nations and dangerous groups such as terrorists. Libertarians are willing to concede that an effective military cannot be privatized and therefore must remain as a function of government.

- Operating the justice system, to protect us from domestic criminals by means of police, courts, jails and government lawyers such as prosecutors and public defenders.

All remaining activities would remain in the private sector. Our purpose is not to make political judgments. Therefore we neither recommend nor reject the libertarian solution. However, from an economic point of view, the libertarian prescription adds to economic efficiency and to the generation of wealth because it maximizes personal choice and freedom, minimizes coercion, and avoids "the tragedy of the commons" since it avoids public ownership of resources as much as possible.

One of the very best articles ever written on economics is the classic tale with the deceptively simple title "I, Pencil." It is the history of a plain lead pencil, but with a twist. This interesting and fascinating article can be found on the web at the following address: http://www.econlib.org/library/Essays/rdPncl1.html

This article is well worth reading, and it explains clearly why a free enterprise economy is much more productive than a centrally managed economy. Another way to say this is that spontaneous self-organizing order is much more efficient than central planning. That is the essential meaning of Adam Smith's "invisible hand."

Motives versus Results

---

[3] These activities cannot be performed in the private sector because of "free riders." There are free riders because the benefits cannot be withheld from people who do not pay for them. Everyone enjoys protection from foreign attack and domestic crime, whether or not they pay for this protection.

A friend tells me of her struggle in being surrounded by people with a different world-view – people who make her feel that in defending liberty, she is greedy, selfish, and uncaring. Are you greedy, selfish, and uncaring? I know that I can be. We all are at times perhaps. Even people who oppose liberty are. But I don't think self-interest explains her view of the proper role of government intervention.

It is probably not surprising to worry about our motives. In our daily interactions, motives are nearly everything. We all want friends and family that care about us, along with their own concerns.

So we pay a lot of attention to motives because they're important. But the motives of strangers are much less important than our own. For one thing, by definition, it is hard to know strangers as well as our families and friends. So the motives of strangers will be much harder to read. But there is a much worse problem which is that, by definition, strangers don't have much information or knowledge of my needs, desires, and dreams. They can't, because they are strangers. It is hard enough for my family and friends to know me well. But strangers cannot know me at all well. So, even with the best of motives, strangers may not be able to help me. In fact, they may end up hurting me despite their good motives. We know that we sometimes hurt our families and friends even with the best of motives because of our imperfect knowledge of who they are.

This suggests we should be humble about intervening in the lives of strangers. Those on the other side of the spectrum of government intervention often lack this humility. They claim to know what is best for others–what they should eat, how they should behave, whether they purchase health insurance, and what is the best use of their money. When their well-intended plans fail, and even cause harm to those they would help, they fall back on their motives – after all, they meant well.

But when dealing with strangers, with people outside our circle of family and friends, results trump motives. Or at least they do for me. That is because I also have good motives. I simply believe, perhaps foolishly, that sometimes it is better to leave things alone than to intervene. Not always - just sometimes. We know that is often true in public policy, just as it is true in parenting, where the motives are very powerful. Sometimes good parenting means letting children make mistakes and learn from those mistakes. Sometimes it means letting children come to grips with personal responsibility.

For example, we teach our children to drive and let them take the car. We know it may be dangerous, but we accept the risk. We do so not because we do not care about our children. It is actually just the opposite. We accept the risk because we care so much about them. We respect them. We want them to leave the nest, and learn to fly on their own.

So my opposition to a minimum wage or government schools or agricultural price supports or bank bailouts or mandatory health insurance or mandatory retirement contributions or mandatory eating habits doesn't come from my selfishness or greed. Rather, these attitudes come from respect for my fellow human beings, and a belief that leaving people free to choose what is best for themselves usually works out better than strangers making decisions for them.

The other day a friend of mine was defending a regulation related to smoking. I hate smoking, even though I used to smoke years ago. But I think people should be free to smoke if they want, and I believe that private establishments – restaurants and apartment buildings and businesses – should be free to allow people to smoke on their premises. My friend does not agree. He is a good person, and knows as I do, that smoking has very serious health consequences. But he feels very self-righteous about regulating smoking even more fully than we currently do. Part of that self-righteousness comes from his motives. He knows they are pure - and they are. I very much respect him. He also happens to be overweight. I wonder how he would feel if I told him that I have been reading a lot lately on diet and health and that I thought he should eat fewer carbohydrates and spend more time at the gym. I think it would be good for him to lose weight. But I would never want to force him to change his habits. Even more than that, my respect for him would keep me from making the suggestion. I think he definitely knows that he is overweight.

He is not a close friend. He is a casual friend. With a very close friend or a sibling, I might say something about the virtues of diet and exercise. But a stranger? I cannot imagine going up to a stranger on the street and lecturing him about his weight. Pushing a stranger to do something about his weight is even harder to imagine. But I do not think my motives are the issue. It's a question of respect, and imperfect knowledge of his feelings.

Those of us who want smaller government because we think it will make the world a better place are the allies, whether we like it or not, of purely selfish people who want smaller government in order to avoid taxes, and who have no intention of giving money to charity. That should give us pause. At the same time, those who care so much about others that they would run their lives for them are allied with those who would run the lives of others because of less attractive motives – for power and profit.

So don't lose any sleep over your motives. And don't let others who are no better than you are, convince you that there is something wrong with you because you do not want to use the power of the state to try to improve the lives of others. Their strategy has a very mixed track record. They always say that this time it will be different. But it is unlikely to be different because of the knowledge problem, and because the other side centralizes power. And centralized power doesn't attract nice people. Just the opposite, in fact. Both sides want to make the world a better place. We just disagree on how to get there.

Chapter Summary

- Price controls come in two varieties. Price floors and price ceilings.

- Price floors create surpluses and price ceilings cause shortages.

- Price controls, whether they are ceilings or price floors, interfere with voluntary exchanges and create shortages, or surpluses or lead to black markets, underground activities, and criminal behavior. Free market prices lead to coordinated supply and demand so that markets clear and the economy is efficient.

- Other forms of government interference in markets, include subsidies and taxes (such as sales taxes, excise taxes and customs duties). Subsidies will create surpluses, because when some good or service is subsidized more of it is supplied. Taxes cause shortages.

- When resources are not privately owned, they are not priced by the free market and tend to be inefficiently allocated. That opens the door to the tragedy of the commons. People who own property take good care of it in their own self-interest. But property that is not privately owned is not taken good care of, because no-one has the incentive to do so.

- This supports the libertarian argument that all resources should be privately owned so far as possible. The government should own and operate resources only when private ownership is impossible, in cases like the military and the justice system.

- Private ownership in a free enterprise economy is more productive than public ownership in a centrally managed economy.

Discussion Questions

1. Which of the following are price floors and which are price ceilings?

    a. Rent controls?

    b. Agricultural price supports?

    c. Medicare and Medicaid reimbursements to health care providers?

    d. Anti price-gouging laws?

    e. The minimum wage?

    f. Speeding fines?

2. Do price floors cause shortages or surpluses? Do price ceilings cause shortages or surpluses?

3. Property is well-maintained when it is privately or publicly owned?

4. What is the remedy for the tragedy of the commons? Is it:

- A government tax?
- A government subsidy?
- Or something entirely different?

5. To promote economic efficiency, which resources should be:
- Publicly owned?

- Privately owned?

6. What is the optimal role of government? Should government do as much or as little as possible? Why?

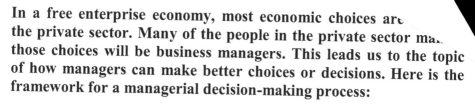

Chapter 7: Management J

It's not hard to make decisions when you kno.
Roy Disney

In a free enterprise economy, most economic choices are the private sector. Many of the people in the private sector ma. those choices will be business managers. This leads us to the topic of how managers can make better choices or decisions. Here is the framework for a managerial decision-making process:

1. Identify the alternatives.

Each decision must have at least two alternatives otherwise there would be no necessity to make a decision.

2. Identify all benefits and costs for each alternative.

Each alternative has certain positive benefits, some of which may be monetary while others may be non-monetary. Also, each alternative has certain negative consequences, called costs, which usually require a monetary payment.

3. Explicitly state all assumptions.

Throughout any decision making process, assumptions must be made. Assumptions are always necessary because we are never be able to cost- effectively collect all of the information we may need to make a fully informed decision. Assumptions cannot be haphazard, but should be reasonable, and should be consistent with available factual evidence.

4. Quantify the benefits and costs.

We must quantify all benefits and costs so that we can compare them. Remember to ignore "sunk costs" (discussed earlier, on p. 42). Usually it is simpler to quantify costs than benefits. But sometimes costs can be difficult or virtually impossible to quantify. For example, if a product has to be recalled due to a defect, then putation of the manufacturer will probably be harmed, and re sales of that product may decline. The damaged reputation d sales decline are certainly costs of the recall. But it will be ifficult to quantify those costs. It can also be difficult or virtually impossible to quantify some benefits. In our example of the recall of a defective product, the reputation of the manufacturer may actually benefit if the manufacturer quickly admits that it is at fault, and speedily acts to recall the product. But the benefit to the manufacturer's reputation of the prompt admission of fault and of the speedy recall may be difficult to quantify.

Despite the difficulties that may arise in quantifying some costs and some benefits, it still remains important to quantify costs and benefits as much as possible, and to find methods of dealing with those costs and benefits which are difficult or even impossible to quantify. These methods do exist, but are too complex to detail here. So we will not discuss them any further, but we should remember that they do exist if we are ever confronted with the need to quantify costs and benefits which are difficult or even impossible to quantify.

5. <u>Compare the benefits and costs of each alternative against the next best alternative</u>.

In economic terminology the next best alternative is characterized as the opportunity cost of the alternative under consideration. The best way to think about this is that the opportunity cost represents what you would have to give up in terms of net benefits if you accept the alternative under consideration. For example, imagine that we are comparing two investment opportunities of similar risk, with Investment A offering an expected return of 15% and Investment B offering an expected return of 12%. We can either select Investment A or Investment B, but not both. Then the opportunity cost of selecting Investment A will be the expected return of 12% on Investment B that we will sacrifice in order to accept Investment A.

6. Finally, select the alternative that adds the most economic value.

This simply means select the opportunity for which the value of the benefits less the costs is greatest. In summary, this is what management decision making is all about.

Effective management decisions require careful comparison of the costs and benefits of alternative actions. For example, all organizations face decisions like:

- Should we make or buy the various components used in our line of products?
- Should we own or rent our business premises?
- Should we employ our own sales force, or should we distribute our products through independent manufacturers' representatives?
- Should we open new branches or should we franchise branches out to individual branch owners?
- Should we write our own software or should we buy canned software off the shelf?
- Should we expand into India on our own, or do we need a joint venture partner?
- And the list goes on and on.

Social responsibility versus profit maximization

Some people contrast social responsibility versus profit maximization, or the limitations of rational analysis due to qualitative factors, such as culture or non-monetary factors, such as preference for leisure time. There is sometimes a suspicion about profit maximization, a caution that it might be too self-seeking, or too ruthless, to be consistent with our broad social values and the public good.

However, many of these qualitative factors are consistent with, and can be taken into account by, profit maximization.

The issue being raised is long-term versus short-term profit maximization. In the short-term monetary and quantitative factors may well crowd out qualitative factors. The urgent often drives out the important. It is hard to be contemplative, wise, kind and thoughtful when in a rush or under pressure. Short-term thinking can be myopic.

But in the long-term short-term tactics will endanger profit maximization. There will be repercussions if a company exploits customers, employees, suppliers, or investors or treats people without proper concern, respect and courtesy.

Companies that are socially irresponsible will face consequences. Unprincipled and unethical behavior will provoke resistance and retribution. So, by considering profit maximization to be long-term rather than short-term, many, if not most, of the qualitative factors can come under the umbrella of profit maximization, and be consistent with profit maximization, rather than being an opposing or "either-or" choice. In a nutshell, there is truth to the popular saying "what goes around comes around."

Consequences of Management Decisions

A large modern corporation requires vast amounts of capital. These vast amounts are too large to be funded by a single individual or even a single family or partnership. Therefore corporations raise capital by selling stocks and bonds to individuals, firms, mutual funds, pension funds, unions, and other organizations.

These owners of the stocks and bonds of any large corporation are numerous, unorganized and geographically widely scattered. They cannot possibly operate the business of the corporation, and are compelled to hire professional managers to do so on their behalf. In order to hold these managers accountable for their actions and to reward or penalize them accordingly, each management is required to issue quarterly and annual financial statements for the corporation under their management. The financial statements are the combined results of the decisions that have been made by each management, and reflect the success or failure of their performance.

It is often said that decisions have consequences. For the decisions of corporate managers, the consequences are shown in the corporate financial statements. Therefore, the corporate financial statements can be considered as the scorecard that reflects the quality and success of management decision-making.

Most of us know the general importance of the "rules of the game" (property rights and the rule of law) to a well-functioning economy. This time we focus in more closely on the "rules of the game" regarding corporate governance and financial reporting. The issue of fraudulent financial reporting relates to the deliberate information distortion by corporate top management that evade its obligations to shareholders, employees, creditors, government, and the general public in order to enrich itself.

Economists call this failure of duty the problem of "agency." Top management is supposed to be the faithful agent of its principal, the shareholders who own the enterprise. But a corrupt agent neglects its duty to its principal in favor of its own selfish interest. Lawyers refer to this same problem as a "conflict of interest." Ethicists see the problem as deviation from moral conduct. But, whatever terminology is used, the problem remains the same: how can the management agency be kept faithful to its duty to the owners, and to the other stakeholders (employees, creditors, government, and the general public)?

This is a fundamental, familiar and difficult problem. The founders of the United States confronted it in attempting to create a federal government that would be powerful enough to perform its functions, but not so powerful that it would become as oppressive to Americans as the English government that had been overthrown by the American Revolution. The founders used the Constitution to achieve these objectives by the means of the separation of powers, the Bill of Rights, and various checks and balances.

After the great depression of the 1930's the U.S. government formed the Securities and Exchange Commission (SEC) to oversee the U.S. financial markets. The basic policy of the SEC has been to promote transparency in corporate finance by requiring corporations to make full disclosure of their financial performance to their stockholders and bondholders. The guiding concept is that "sunshine is the best disinfectant." Among the devices used to create the sunshine of full disclosure are the legal requirements for public companies to issue quarterly financial statements, reviewed[7] by independent auditors, and annual financial statements subject to compulsory audits.

The benefits to society from financial transparency are efficient capital markets that link investors with businesses seeking funds. Efficient capital markets lower the cost of capital by reducing the risks to investors from fraud and from other undisclosed business hazards. When financial reporting becomes corrupted, capital markets lose efficiency, and the cost of capital increases due to the increased risks.

Under the full disclosure approach, independent auditors, corporate directors (especially independent directors), and the SEC are key players that serve as checks and balances on corrupt top managements and that provide the sunshine that disinfects. Unfortunately, in recent years independent auditors, corporate directors (especially independent directors), and the SEC have sometimes failed to play their important roles, and many corporate top managements have become dominant and unrestrained. This increasing power and lack of restraint of corporate top managements has been evidenced in many ways, including the following:

- Exorbitant executive pay, including vastly excessive salaries, bonuses, and "perks."

- Large increases in executive pay despite poor corporate

---

7 A "Review" is an examination by an auditor that is less extensive than an audit, and which therefore provides a lesser degree of assurance than a full audit.

financial performance or even the incurring of losses.

- Repricing of "underwater" stock options to more favorable terms, even in the face of declining financial results.

- "Evergreen" stock option plans that are renewed without stockholder approval

- Boards of directors who are handpicked by top management to be docile, and who are seduced by lavish pay, lush benefits, generous "perks", and lordly privileges.

- The "race to the bottom" where corporations register in states (such as Delaware) that have the most lax corporate laws and that make it difficult for reformers to sue or challenge corporation managements.

- Adoption of corporate devices such as "poison pills", "golden parachutes", "golden handcuffs", "white knights", "greenmail", and staggered terms of office for directors in order to insulate and protect incumbent management from corporate raiders and dissident investors.

The increasing percentage of corporate securities being held by passive institutional investors such as public and private pension funds, mutual funds, trusts and foundations, college and university endowment funds, and other organizations that feel no incentive or experience no pressure to oppose corporate top managements that are not maximizing stockholder value.

Auditors have a clear and compelling duty to report honestly, and to resist management pressure to close their eyes to fraudulent financial reporting. But, in some cases, auditors have buckled under or - even worse – actually facilitated fraudulent financial reporting. There is no excuse for these lapses. But, from a pragmatic point of view, they cannot be unexpected when some corporate directors have become CEO poodles, and the SEC has all too often fallen asleep at the switch. Despite the failures of directors and regulators to act as and when they should, it is hoped that CPA's will do their moral duty. However, it is realistic to fear that some CPA's will fall short as watchdogs, and turn into lapdogs.

Are there signs that can foretell that financial statements are being materially misstated? There is no sure-fire indicator. But there are clues that can warn one of potential trouble ahead. Here are some examples:

- Watch out for companies that have a unbroken string of steadily improving earnings per share. But isn't this a desirable thing? Yes, but not when it becomes imperative for management to keep the string going in order to stay in office and keep stockholders satisfied and quiet. That is a slippery slope that can lead to fraudulent financial reporting.

- Be alert for major acquisitions made by means of exchanges of stock, rather than for cash. For one thing, research has shown that stock mergers are considerably less successful over time than cash mergers. When real cash is on the line there is more pressure to succeed than when only paper is used as a currency for a merger. For another thing, when stock is used as a currency for acquisitions, management has a powerful incentive to boost the stock price in order to enhance the value of their currency and make bigger acquisitions. Unfortunately one of the quickest and easiest ways to boost the stock price in a hurry is to inflate earnings by fraud.

- Be wary of boards of directors that include celebrities (such as retired generals, politicians, professional athletes, and entertainers – all of whom may lack business experience), or CEO's of other companies (who may sit on each other's boards or have other reasons to turn a blind eye or not to rock the boat when push comes to shove). And be wary of CEO's who frequently appear on TV, or play in celebrity golf tournaments, or serve on more than one or two boards of trustees of charities, universities, hospitals, or foundations. CEO's are paid to run their companies, not to bask in publicity or hobnob with the rich and famous.

- Exorbitant executive pay, including vastly excessive salaries, bonuses, and "perks." Exorbitant executive is evidence of a weak board of directors and a dominating CEO: a toxic combination.

- Large increases in executive pay despite poor corporate financial performance or even the incurring of losses. This too may be evidence of a weak board of directors and a dominating CEO.

- Repricing of "underwater" stock options to more favorable terms, even in the face of declining financial results. May be further evidence of a weak board of directors and a dominating CEO.

- "Evergreen" stock option plans that are renewed without stockholder approval. May be additional evidence of a weak board of directors and a dominating CEO

- Adoption of corporate devices such as "poison pills", "golden parachutes", "golden handcuffs", "white knights", "greenmail", and staggered terms of office for directors in order to insulate and protect incumbent management from corporate raiders[8] and dissident investors. Once again this may be evidence of a weak board of directors and a dominating CEO

- Read financial statement notes very closely, paying attention to:

  - related party transactions (these are dealings that are not at arms length, and are therefore inherently

---

[8] Corporate raiders often perform a useful function. They target underperforming companies in order to acquire them, to cut out lavish management "perks" and manage more efficiently in order to improve returns to investors.

suspect). GAAP[9] requires related party transactions to be disclosed.

- contingencies (which may include pending lawsuits against the company for fraudulent financial reporting),

- management estimates which are of significant importance, such as:

  - profits on major construction contracts, which can take years to complete, and where interim estimated profits can legitimately be recognized, but are tricky to measure and subject to future uncertainties,

  - underground reserves of oil, gas, precious minerals, or coal, which are subject to revision, and which can fluctuate in value when prices fall steeply and unexpectedly,

  - substantial amounts of loans receivable, which may not be fully collectible if borrowers are corrupt, unstable or lack financial substance (for example, bank loans to countries with corrupt or insecure regimes – think of the problems the French and Russians are having with getting repaid on their large loans to Iraq).

---

9 GAAP stands for Generally Accepted Accounting Principles, which are the rules required by law for presenting financial information. The main purpose of GAAP is to ensure that financial statements are uniform in nature, so that the financial statements of one firm can be compared to that firm's financial statements for earlier periods, and to the financial statements of other firms, especially other firms that are competitors in the same industry.

- Analyze financial statements and ratios very thoroughly. In particular, watch out for cases where cash from operations is falling as a percentage of funds for financing investment in the business, and cash from outside financing is a rising percentage funds for financing investment in the business. Also be vigilant for declining short term solvency (such as deteriorating current and quick ratios, and slowing turnover of receivables, inventories, and payables). The reason? When companies fraudulently inflate reported earnings, there is no corresponding increase in cash flow. So there is an increasing need for outside funds to prop up the company.

- We hear a lot about systems of internal control. These are various checks and balances designed to prevent fraud and to protect corporate assets. Examples of checks and balances are:

  - Requiring not one but two signatures on all company checks;

  - Rotation of duties, so that any employee who is committing fraud gets rotated out of that position before they can operate long term;

  - Separation of duties, so that someone who writes out purchase orders does not write checks to pay suppliers – which prevents someone from writing fake purchase orders followed by writing payment checks that they steal and deposit in their own bank account;

  - Requiring authorization of all expenditures above a certain limit, such as $5,000, in order to prevent unauthorized expenditures;

But be aware that internal controls can be defeated, especially when:

- Two or more employees collaborate, or

- Top management overrides the controls, as has happened in some of the very big frauds like Adelphia, Enron, Sunbeam, Tyco and WorldCom.

- Avoid companies that publish "pro forma" earnings. GAAP earnings are the legally required standard for measuring earnings. "Pro forma" earnings are a device to make disappointing GAAP earnings look better. They are cosmetics designed to cover flaws and blemishes. Managements who publish "pro forma" earnings are not trying to communicate, but to obfuscate. This is a clear red flag. Don't stand for it.

- Last, but not least, do not invest in stocks of only a very few companies. If just one of these companies is a future Enron, you will incur a substantial loss. So be sure to broadly diversify your stock investments. Often an index fund is the best choice for investing in stocks. Good index funds usually beat more than 80% of actively managed stock mutual funds. And high-performing stock mutual funds in one year seldom continue to be high performers in following years. Rather, they tend to revert to the mean – which is inferior to good index funds.

Chapter Summary

- A framework for management decision-making is as follows:
  - Identify the alternatives
  - Identify all benefits and costs for each alternative
  - Explicitly state all assumptions
  - Quantify the benefits and costs
  - Compare the benefits and costs of each alternative against the next best alternative.
  - Finally, select the alternative that adds the most economic value.

- The issue of social responsibility versus profit maximization can be reconciled, if one considers the long term.

- The corporate financial statements can be considered as the scorecard that reflects the quality and success of management decision-making.

- Problems with corporate financial reporting can erode the rule of law, unless laws are consistent with economic incentives and ethical conduct.

- There are clear symptoms of unethical behavior, such as:

  1. Exorbitant executive pay, despite poor corporate financial performance
  2. Repricing of "underwater" stock options to more favorable terms
  3. Adoption of corporate devices such as "poison pills"
  4. An unbroken string of steadily improving earnings per share
  5. Major acquisitions made by means of exchanges of stock, rather than for cash
  6. Boards of directors that include celebrities from fields such as entertainment, sports or politics

Discussion Questions

1. Put the following steps in cost-benefit analysis into their correct order:

   - Quantify the benefits and costs

   - Select the alternative that adds the most economic value.

   - Identify all benefits and costs for each alternative

   - Identify the alternatives
   - Explicitly state all assumptions

   - Compare the benefits and costs of each alternative against the next best alternative.

2. Can the issue of social responsibility versus profit maximization be reconciled? If so, how?

3. Are the results of management decisions displayed on a kind of scorecard?

4. How does fraudulent financial reporting affect the rule of law, and secure property rights?

5. What are five symptoms that can reveal management fraud?

6. Are there flaws in internal control systems? If so, are internal control systems useless?

Chapter 8: Globalization

A lie can travel half way around the world while the truth is putting on its shoes.

Mark Twain

In an earlier chapter we discussed how specialization stimulates trade. But we have still to discuss who specializes in what, and why. Consider the following example. Jack and Jill are shipwrecked on a desert island. Fortunately there are coconut palms on the island and clams to be gathered on the beach. Jack can pick 12 coconuts in an hour or find 10 clams in an hour. Jill can pick only 9 coconuts in an hour, but she can find 14 clams in an hour.

Clearly Jack is better at picking coconuts, and Jill is better at catching clams. Therefore both are better off if Jack specializes in picking coconuts while Jill finds clams. Jack's skill at picking coconuts is what economists call his *comparative advantage*, and Jill's comparative advantage is her skill at catching clams. Since each has specialized, they will trade coconuts for clams.

When each specializes according to their comparative advantage, and they trade coconuts for clams, both are both better off and the situation is Pareto-efficient. We have learned that people specialize in whatever happens to be their comparative advantage and then trade with other specialists in order to obtain other goods and services. By means of trade all parties become better off in this Pareto-efficient process, as shown in Tables 8-1 and 8-2.

Table 8-1

Example with Specialization

Name	Coconuts per hour	Clams per hour	Specialized Coconuts	Specialized Clams
Jack	12	10	12	
Jill	10	14		14
Average	11	12	12	14

As Table 8-1 shows, with specialization, Jack and Jill together get 12 coconuts and 14 clams.

Table 8-2

No Specialization	Name	Coconuts per hour	Clams per hour	Not Specialized Total Coconuts	Not Specialized Total Clams
½ hour for Coconuts & ½ hour for Clams	Jack	12	10	6	5
½ hour for Coconuts & ½ hour for Clams	Jill	10	14	5	7
	Total			11	12

As Table 8-2 shows, with no specialization, Jack and Jill each have to pick their own coconuts and dig their own clams. Let us assume that they each spend a half-hour picking coconuts and a half-hour finding clams. Jack and Jill together get only 11 coconuts (compared with 12 coconuts when they specialized) and 12 clams (compared with 14 clams when they specialized). Clearly Jack and Jill got more coconuts as well as more clams when they specialize than when they did not specialize, and had to be self-sufficient.

It is similarly true that entire nations specialize according to their comparative advantage and then trade with various nations in order to obtain other goods and services. For example, the U.S. specializes in jet aircraft, movies, and wheat – all of which it produces in excess of what it consumes, and exports the remainder to other countries. The U.S. imports goods from nations that specialize according to their respective comparative advantages. These imports include automobiles and television sets from Japan and South Korea, coffee from Brazil, and many different items from China. In fact, it has been said that the U.S. grows Toyotas and Hondas in the wheat fields of Iowa – which means that the U.S. ships Midwestern wheat to Japan, and Japan exports autos to the U.S.

So far we have shown that specialization, based upon comparative advantage, leads to increased trade, which in turn helps all parties to become better off in this Pareto-efficient process, regardless of whether these parties are individuals or entire nations, and regardless of whether the trade is only domestic, or crosses national frontiers.

But what if one nation has a comparative advantage in every single good and service, and if all other nations have a comparative disadvantage in every single good and service? In that case, why would the nation that has a comparative advantage in every single good and service want to engage in international trade? In order to answer that question, let us go back to our earlier example of Jack and Jill on their desert island. But this time we assume that Jill has a comparative advantage both in picking coconuts and in catching clams. The details are shown in Table 8-3.

Table 8-3

Example with Special-ization	Name	Coconuts per hour	Clams per hour	Optimal Coconuts	Optimal Clams
Old Example	Jack	12	10	12	
	Jill	10	14		14
	Average	11	12	12	14
New Example	Jack	10	10	10	
	Jill	12	14		14
	Average	11	12	10	14

As Table 8-3 shows, in the new example with specialization, Jack and Jill together get 10 coconuts and 14 clams.

Table 8-4

Example with no Specialization	Name	Coconuts per hour	Clams per hour	Total Coconuts	Total Clams
Old Example	Jack	12	10	6	5
½ hour for Coconuts & ½ hour for Clams	Jill	10	14	5	7
	Total			11	12
New Example	Jack	10	10	5	5
½ hour for Coconuts & ½ hour for Clams	Jill	12	14	6	7
	Total			11	12

As Table 8-4 shows, in the new example with no specialization, Jack and Jill each have to pick their own coconuts and dig their own clams. Let us assume that they each spend a half-hour picking coconuts and a half-hour finding clams. Jack and Jill together get 11 coconuts (compared with 10 coconuts when they specialized) and 12 clams (compared with 14 clams when they specialized). These results are mixed: with no specialization, Jack and Jill gain one coconut more, but two less clams. Are Jack and Jill better off or worse off in this situation? Table 8-5 addresses this question.

Table 8-5

New Example with Specialization

Name	Coconuts per hour	Clams per hour	Opportunity Cost of Coconuts
Jack	10	10	1 Clam
Jill	12	14	14/12 = 1.17 Clams
Average			1.09 Clams
Gain	+1		+1.09 Clams
Loss		-2	-2.00 Clams
Net Loss			-0.91 Clams

In order to answer this question, we need to convert coconuts into the equivalent number of clams. Then we can make a clam-to-clam comparison. As Table 8-5 shows, the opportunity cost of one coconut is 1 clam for Jack, and 1.17 clams for Jill, resulting in an average of 1.09 clams.

With no specialization, Jack and Jill gained 1 coconut = 1.09 clams over the result with specialization. But with no specialization, Jack and Jill lost 2 clams, compared with specialization. The net loss with no specialization, compared with specialization, is 0.91 clams.

That shows that specialization is more efficient than no specialization even when one party has a comparative advantage in all goods and services. It still pays for the country with a comparative advantage in all goods to concentrate on producing those goods where its comparative advantage is greatest, and importing those goods where its comparative advantage is smallest from less efficient countries. In other words, regardless of comparative advantage, specialization and trade are always more economically efficient than self-sufficiency. Therefore globalization is Pareto-optimal, and free trade is always more efficient than protectionism.

Imports and exports make every importing and exporting country better off, and are Pareto-efficient. So we have learned that trade, whether it be domestic or international, is wealth-producing and efficient for all participants, whether they be individuals or countries. Trade is further stimulated and efficient when barriers to trade are removed. These barriers include import and export quotas and restrictions, as well as excise taxes and customs duties. The greatest gains come from the most unrestricted trade, free of import and export quotas and excise taxes and customs duties.

The Political Tendency

The political tendency is for nations to make reciprocal treaties for removing barriers to trade, such as the North American Free Trade Agreement (NAFTA) between Canada, the United States and Mexico. Politicians talk of establishing "a level playing field" whereby countries match each other in lowering barriers to trade. Sometimes these agreements cannot be completed because of sticking points. For example, many nations protect their domestic farmers by banning agricultural imports, or by imposing heavy customs duties on agricultural imports.

Politicians argue convincingly that trade concessions will be made only to countries that offer reciprocal concessions, which sounds fair and reasonable. As fair and reasonable as this may sound, it is faulty logic. We are better off if we unilaterally remove barriers to trade, even if other countries refuse to reciprocate. Of course we are even better off if other countries do reciprocate. But we should not let the perfect be the enemy of the good, and we should realize that half a loaf is better than none. But few people, other than economists, understand this, and so it is not a popular idea.

We can even go further, and become wealthier and more efficient by eliminating another barrier to trade, namely dumping duties. Dumping occurs when some country exports goods to another country at a price that seems too low to be profitable to the exporting country. When so-called dumping appears to take place, cries of indignation arise, along with complaints that evil foreign governments are subsidizing exports in order to ruin our domestic industries.

Politicians then make fiercely patriotic speeches and vote to impose dumping duties on these dumped goods. This is good politics, but faulty economics. If foreigners wish to subsidize exports, we should snap up these bargains with gratitude and enthusiasm, and even urge the foreigners to dump more cheap goods on us so that we can benefit from these discounted prices.

Looking at this issue more closely, we see that consumers of these allegedly dumped goods get the benefit of cheaper prices. But employees of our domestic manufacturers may suffer pay cuts, or layoffs because domestic manufacturers will have to cut prices to compete with the cheap imports. It is these threatened workers, and their employers, who raise the howls of protest against the cheap imports. These protests by the relatively few make news headlines. However, the benefit to the many of cheaper prices from dumping seldom hits the headlines, and is seldom apparent to the public, although it is obvious to economists. Once again, good politics tends to be bad economics.

To the uninformed public, protectionism sounds necessary, and free trade sounds threatening. A good example of this is the widespread opposition to outsourcing. To economists, outsourcing is efficient and wealth-producing. But those opposed to outsourcing protest vehemently about good jobs leaving America and going to India, Bangladesh or Vietnam, where labor costs are much lower, and there are no labor unions to protect workers from being exploited by ruthless capitalists.

On the one hand, it is true that cheap imports and outsourcing will cost some American workers their jobs. But the economic benefits from outsourcing will benefit all American consumers, who vastly outnumber the workers who become victims of cheap imports and outsourcing. Think of the low prices we enjoy at Wal-Mart, which sells a vast array of goods imported from China and other countries where wage levels are well below American wages.

The best economic solution is to give temporary public assistance to displaced workers in order to retrain them for new jobs in sectors of our economy where they can once more be productive and earn good wages. Since free trade benefits all consumers, and since cheap imports harm only a much smaller number of displaced workers, it is clear that the gains from free trade will greatly exceed the costs of retraining displaced workers. In that case, it is both economically efficient and ethical to provide temporary public assistance in order to retrain displaced workers so that they can find new jobs and again become self-supporting. The only obstacle to this sensible economic solution is public ignorance and political appeals to the prejudices and misconceptions of the populace.

Political opponents of globalization often argue as follows:

1. Globalization increases the wealth of rich nations and increases the poverty of poor nations, thus widening the gap between rich and poor;

2. Globalization fosters an environmental "race to the bottom" as large multinational corporations relocate to areas of the world where anti-pollution laws are lax or non-existent, and the result is to cause environmental damage in developing nations;

multinational corporations relocate to areas of the world where workers are poorly paid and ruthlessly exploited as sweated labor and child labor.

4. Globalization is the major cause of job losses and unemployment.

Each of these accusations is not only false, but the opposite is true. It is true that:

1. Globalization increases the wealth of all nations, not just rich nations. It is a rising tide that lifts all boats, large or small. The evidence of growing prosperity in developing countries is widely visible. Think of the impressive economic progress that has taken place over the last 30-40 years in China, India, Taiwan, South Korea, Hong Kong, Singapore, Malaysia, Thailand, Vietnam, Poland, Lithuania, Finland, Spain, Chile, Brazil, Botswana, New Zealand and Dubai.

2. It is only through globalization that poor nations can become better off through trade, and become prosperous enough to afford stricter environmental controls.

3. While labor conditions tend to be harsher in developing countries, workers in developing countries eagerly seek out employment with multinational corporations because these multinational corporations offer better jobs than otherwise available, better working conditions, and better chances of advancement than previously attainable.

4. Globalization is by no means a cause of job losses and unemployment. On the contrary, globalization causes job growth and increases employment.

It is not globalization that destroys jobs. It is technology that is both the major creator of new jobs, and the greatest destroyer of old jobs. For example, think of all the people currently employed in the hardware and software sectors of the personal computer industry. Thirty years ago, there were no personal computers and no jobs in the personal computer industry. On the other hand, think of all the people thirty years ago who were employed as telephone operators, stenographers and typists. Today these jobs hardly exist. Technology is the driving force that creates new jobs and that destroys old jobs.

Chapter Summary

- The theory of comparative advantage explains how individuals and entire countries select to specialize in particular goods and services.

- Specialization, based on comparative advantage, stimulates trade, both domestic and international.

- Trade, both domestic and international, is economically efficient and wealth-producing for all parties.

- Even in the extreme case where one individual or one nation, has the comparative advantage in every kind of goods and services, specialization and trade are still economically efficient and wealth-producing for all parties..

- Barriers to trade, such as import and export restrictions, quotas, protectionism, customs duties, dumping duties, and excise taxes are all economically inefficient and wealth-reducing.

- Politicians favor reciprocal trade agreements, and demand that concessions by one country should be matched by other countries, whereas economics makes it clear that unilateral reduction of barriers to trade is economically efficient and wealth-producing for the country that unilaterally lowers barriers to trade.

- It is very clear that international trade is economically efficient and wealth-producing for all parties. But the public tends to favor protectionism and the imposition of dumping duties, and to condemn outsourcing, due to public ignorance and political appeals to the prejudices and misconceptions of the populace.

- While globalization and free trade benefit the many, they can cause distress to some workers who lose their jobs to cheap imports. Since the gains from free trade vastly exceed the losses to the few workers, it is economically efficient and ethical to provide public assistance in order to retrain displaced workers, and help them to obtain new jobs.

- Globalization is resisted and often opposed by politicians who falsely blame globalization for a host of problems. In each case, globalization is actually beneficial to all parties, and harmful to very few, if any, parties.

- Globalization is mistakenly blamed for destroying jobs, when it actually creates jobs. But the job impact of globalization pales compared to the job impact of technology. Technology is by far the greatest force in creating new jobs, and in destroying old jobs.

Discussion Questions

1. Think of yourself as engaged in trade. First, who do you sell the most to? If you are working in a job, could your biggest customer be your employer, to whom you sell your labor services. Who is your biggest supplier? Could it be your supermarket that sells you groceries, or is it perhaps your landlord, who sells you housing?

2. How much are you participating in globalization? For example, where were the following items manufactured:

- Your TV?
- Your cell phone?
- Your toaster?
- Your shirt?
- Your shoes?
- Your computer?
- Your furniture?
- Your jeans?
- Your tennis racket or golf clubs or swimsuit or skis?

3. How difficult is it to find imported fruit or produce in your supermarket? Where do your bananas, grapes, peaches, melons, and pineapples come from? And where do your tomatoes, lettuce, avocados and Brussels sprouts come from?

4. Should illegal immigrants be given deportation orders, jail terms, welfare, social security benefits, amnesty or jobs?

5. Why are prescription drugs cheaper in Canada than in the U.S. and yet cheaper in Mexico?

6. If prescription drugs are cheaper in Canada, why doesn't some entrepreneur buy them in Canada and resell them in the U.S. at a profit?

Chapter 9: Book Summary

This chapter is intended to pull together the threads of the entire book. We begin by reproducing the summaries from the end of each chapter below. Then we will condense the main ideas into just a few major themes.

Summary of Chapter 1: Introduction

- Much of the world suffers from extreme scarcity of resources and deep poverty.
- How have some nations progressed towards less scarcity and greater prosperity?
- By means of the rule of law and secure property rights.
- Under the rule of law and secure property rights, people make free choices that increase individual and collective wealth.
- The result is a competitive and efficient economy, where trade makes everyone better off.

Summary of Chapter 2: Specialization, Trade and Prosperity

- Specialization allows people to become more productive and more prosperous than if they were self-sufficient.
- The more specialized one becomes, the more one depends on others to supply one's needs.
- By means of the rule of law and secure property rights.
- Under the rule of law and secure property rights, people are more able to specialize, and make free choices that increase individual and collective wealth.
- The result is a competitive and efficient economy, where trade makes everyone better off.

Summary of Chapter 3: Demand for Goods and Services

- Effective demand means the quantity is actually purchased, not just what consumers might desire.
- Demand varies with price. The Law of Demand states: the lower the price, the greater the quantity demanded.
- Scarcity means that there must be rationing of goods and services.
- Rationing can be done by:
    - Physical quotas: x pairs of shoes per year.
    - Favoritism or patronage: only the nobility are allowed to hunt deer or eat venison.
    - Prices: whoever has the money can buy the goods.
- Rationing by quota is inefficient because it restricts personal freedom to choose, and it results in corruption, crime, black markets, and other ways to game the system.
- Rationing by favoritism or patronage destroys the incentive of common people to work hard or to be creative, because whatever they produce by hard work or creativity will be confiscated and enjoyed by the ruling elite
- Rationing by price is efficient because it generates voluntary exchanges, which increase the wealth of all participants, and result in an efficient economy.
- The price elasticity of demand states how the quantity demanded changes in relation to price.
- Price elasticity of demand depends largely on the availability of substitutes.
- Price elasticity of demand is used in business to charge higher prices to customers with inelastic demand and lower prices to customers with elastic demand.
- The availability of substitutes determines the degree of market power wielded by suppliers.

Summary of Chapter 4: The Supply of Goods and Services

- Cost is a sacrifice of resources, usually made in order to obtain a more highly valued good or service.

- Explicit costs are actual payments made, and implicit costs are sacrifices of other opportunities, known as opportunity costs.
- Relevant costs are those costs affected by any particular choice. Therefore relevant costs are incremental or marginal costs, which are the additional costs caused by the decision under consideration.
- Sunk costs are never relevant, and are costs already incurred, and therefore not affected by the decision under consideration.
- Supply curves are plots of supply quantities against the total cost of each quantity supplied.
- The Law of Supply states that the quantity supplied will increase as the price increases – as opposed to the Law of Demand, which states that the quantity demanded will decrease as the price increases.
- Suppliers will sell at higher prices to customer segments with inelastic demand, and at lower prices to customer segments with elastic demand.

Summary of Chapter 5: Supply and Demand

- A market is any arrangement where buyers and sellers can makes exchanges.
- Middlemen are important participants in markets, because they serve several purposes, such as facilitating contacts between buyers and sellers, and reducing transaction costs.
- Middlemen are not parasites. They can be eliminated, but their functions can never be eliminated.
- Free markets are automatically self-adjusting and self-clearing through operation of the price mechanism.
- When a society interferes with these price signals, by curtailing free markets in favor of centralized planning, price signals are lost. Then supply and demand become uncoordinated and the results are shortages and surpluses.
- Externalities interfere with price signals and reduce

efficiency. It is best to avoid imposing coercive solutions like laws that ban pollution and other negative externalities. A more flexible approach, such as a tax on pollution, is preferable in order to internalize the externality, and thereby to restore the functioning of the price mechanism

Summary of Chapter 6: Supply and Demand Issues

- Price controls come in two varieties. Price floors and price ceilings.
- Price floors create surpluses and price ceilings cause shortages.
- Price controls, whether they are ceilings or price floors, interfere with voluntary exchanges and create shortages, or surpluses or lead to black markets, underground activities, and criminal behavior. Free market prices lead to coordinated supply and demand so that markets clear and the economy is efficient.

- Other forms of government interference in markets include subsidies and taxes (such as sales taxes, excise taxes and customs duties). Subsidies will create surpluses, because when some good or service is subsidized more of it is supplied. Taxes cause shortages.
- When resources are not privately owned, they are not priced by the free market and tend to be inefficiently allocated. That opens the door to the tragedy of the commons. People who own property take good care of it in their own self-interest. But property that is not privately owned is not taken good care of, because no-one has the incentive to do so.
- This supports the libertarian argument that all resources should be privately owned so far as possible. The government should own and operate resources only when private ownership is impossible, in cases like the military and the justice system.
- Private ownership in a free enterprise economy is much

more productive than public ownership in a centrally managed economy.

Summary of Chapter 7: Management Decision-making

- A framework for management decision-making is as follows:
    1. Identify the alternatives
    2. Identify all benefits and costs for each alternative
    3. Explicitly state all assumptions
    4. Quantify the benefits and costs
    5. Compare the benefits and costs of each alternative against the next best alternative.
    6. Finally, select the alternative that adds the most economic value.

- The issue of social responsibility versus profit maximization can be reconciled, if one considers the long term.

- The corporate financial statements can be considered as the scorecard that reflects the quality and success of management decision-making.

- Problems with corporate financial reporting can erode the rule of law, unless laws are consistent with economic incentives and ethical conduct.

- There are clear symptoms of unethical behavior, such as:
    1. Exorbitant executive pay, despite poor corporate financial performance
    2. Repricing of "underwater" stock options to more favorable terms
    3. Adoption of corporate devices such as "poison pills"
    4. An unbroken string of steadily improving earnings per share
    5. Major acquisitions made by means of exchanges of stock, rather than for cash
    6. Boards of directors that include celebrities from fields such as entertainment, sports or politics

Summary of Chapter 8: Globalization

- The theory of comparative advantage explains how individuals and entire countries select to specialize in particular goods and services.

- Specialization, based on comparative advantage, stimulates trade, both domestic and international.
- Trade, both domestic and international, is economically efficient and wealth-producing for all parties.
- Even in the extreme case where one individual or one nation, has the comparative advantage in every kind of goods and services, specialization and trade are still economically efficient and wealth-producing for all parties.
- Barriers to trade, such as import and export restrictions, quotas, protectionism, customs duties, dumping duties, and excise taxes are all economically inefficient and wealth-reducing.
- Politicians favor reciprocal trade agreements, and demand that concessions by one country should be matched by other countries, whereas economics makes it clear that unilateral reduction of barriers to trade is economically efficient and wealth-producing for the country that unilaterally lowers barriers to trade.
- It is very clear that international trade is economically efficient and wealth-producing for all parties. But the public tends to favor protectionism and the imposition of dumping duties, and to condemn outsourcing, due to public ignorance and political appeals to the prejudices and misconceptions of the populace.
- While globalization and free trade benefit the many, they can cause distress to some workers who lose their jobs to cheap imports. Since the gains from free trade vastly exceed the losses to the few workers, it is economically efficient and ethical to provide public assistance in order to retrain

displaced workers, and help them to obtain new jobs.
- Globalization is resisted and often opposed by politicians who falsely blame globalization for a host of problems. In each case, globalization is actually beneficial to all parties, and harmful to very few, if any, parties.
- Globalization is mistakenly blamed for destroying jobs, when it actually creates jobs. But the job impact of globalization pales compared to the job impact of technology. Technology is by far the greatest force in creating new jobs, and in destroying old jobs.

Major Themes

All of the points above can be distilled into a few major themes, as shown below.

A. Personal Rights and Responsibilities

For an economy to function efficiently, each individual consumer and supplier needs to pay the cost and reap the benefit for every transaction in which they participate. The reason is that people are more careful about spending their own money than about spending other peoples' money. We take better care of our own property than a stranger would. As the saying goes: "no-one waxes a rental car."

B. Other Peoples' Money

All transactions done by the government involve spending other peoples' money, which is collected under coercion rather than as a voluntary free choice. Free choices are efficient and wealth-producing. But that cannot be said about coerced actions. Therefore coerced actions should be avoided as much as possible. When an individual or a business in the private sector makes a successful decision they get the profit, but if they make an unsuccessful decision, they bear the loss. But, government officials receive no profit for making successful decisions and do not bear the losses resulting from unsuccessful decisions. Since self-interest and profit or loss are powerful incentives, it follows that all transactions should take place in the private sector, except those that absolutely positively can only be done by government, namely operating the military and the criminal justice system.

C. Incentives

Economics is based on self-interest. Therefore incentives drive behavior. In a competitive free market economy the profit incentive drives thrift, investment and innovation, which create prosperity. But if the incentives are derailed by price controls, quotas, taxes or other government interference with the price system then there will be shortages, surpluses, black markets and increased crime.

D. Freedom of Choice

Freedom of choice is not unlimited license for any kind of conduct. Freedom of choice must be constrained by the rule of law, including secure property rights. But the rule of law should be the one and only limit on free choice. Under free choice the customer is king, and suppliers will find ways to profit by giving people what they want. We need to maximize opportunity, and to minimize mandatory direction of behavior.

E. Welfare

Compassion for the ill, the disabled and those in distress is a virtue. But compassion should extend only to those truly in need and only for their time of need. Public assistance should not only lift up the fallen, but should assist them to stand on their own feet as soon as possible. If charity extends beyond true need, then it erodes initiative, self-discipline and honesty. When carried too far, compassion and charity can create welfare dependency, laziness and moral hazard.

F. Seen and Unseen

The public and politicians react to what is seen. For example, when U.S. steel mills are driven out of business by cheaper steel imports from Asia, what is seen are the workers who lost their jobs, and are now unemployed. What is unseen are the lower prices that consumers will pay for products that contain steel, from autos to tools to eating utensils.

When a hurricane devastates a city, what is seen are the destroyed houses, fallen trees and homeless residents. What is unseen are the delays in repairing damaged property due to price-gouging laws, which outlaw price increases that would attract quick deliveries of building supplies from areas unaffected by the hurricane.

The chief difference between the public and the politicians, on the one hand, and economists, on the other hand, is that the public and the politicians react only to what is seen. Economists also consider what is not seen.

Suggestions for Further Reading

The following books are lively, interesting, informative and well-written in easy-to-understand, non-technical language.

Applied Economics: 2nd Edition. Thinking Beyond Stage One, by Thomas Sowell, Basic Books (2008).

Basic Economics: 3rd Edition. A Common Sense Guide to the Economy, by Thomas Sowell, Basic Books (2007)

The Housing Boom and Bust, by Thomas Sowell, Basic Books (2009).

Liberty Versus the Tyranny of Socialism: Controversial Essays, by Walter Williams, Hoover Institution Press (2008).

Government Failure Versus Market Failure, by Clifford Winston, AEI-Brookings Joint Center for Regulatory Studies (2006)

The Baseball Economist, by J.C. Bradbury, Dutton (2007)

The Birth of Plenty, by William J. Bernstein, McGraw-Hill (2004)

The Choice, by Russell Roberts, Prentice-Hall (2001)

Glossary of Economic Terms

- **Balance of Trade**: the monetary amount of a country's exports less the monetary amount of its imports.

- **Coercion**: the use or threat of force rather than voluntary choice in order to compel a desired action to be taken.

- **Comparative Advantage**: being able to produce a good or service at a lower opportunity cost than another party.

- **Competition:** the existence of many buyers and sellers in the market for a specific good or service, with no buyer or seller having much greater market power than the remaining buyers and sellers.

- **Demand**: the quantity of a given good or service that will be bought at a specific price.

- **Economics**: the scientific study of how choices relating to goods and services are made, and the related consequences, intended and unintended.

- **Economy:** the various markets and non-market processes by which resources are allocated and goods and services are provided and rationed.

- **Efficiency:** choices for which the benefits exceed the costs.

- **Elasticity:** the response of the quantity of any good or service to a change in its price.

- **Externality:** the cost or benefit that third parties unintentionally obtain from activities in which they have not participated.

- <u>Good:</u> anything that is demanded because its benefit exceeds its cost (as opposed to a bad, which has a cost greater than its benefit).

- <u>Inferior Good</u>: anything of which more is demanded when its price has not decreased.

- <u>Law of Demand</u>: the quantity demanded of any good will increase (decrease) when its price decreases (increases).

- <u>Law of Supply:</u> the quantity supplied of any good will decrease (increase) when its price decreases (increases).

- <u>Marginal:</u> incremental.

- <u>Market:</u> any means or process of exchanging goods and services.

- <u>Middleman:</u> any party whose function is to reduce transaction costs.

- <u>Minimum Wage</u>: the floor price for labor required by law.

- <u>Money</u>: a general or universal medium of exchange for buying or selling goods or services.

- <u>Monopoly</u>: when there is only a single seller in a market.

- <u>Monopsony</u>: when there is only a single buyer in a market.

- <u>Opportunity Cost</u>: the next best choice that is sacrificed in order to take a preferred choice.

- <u>Price Ceiling</u>: a maximum price required by law.

- <u>Price Control</u>: a price floor or ceiling mandated by law.

- **Price Floor**: a minimum price required by law.

- **Price Maker**: a market participant with sufficient market power to affect the ruling price.

- **Price Taker**: a market participant with insufficient market power to affect the ruling price.

- **Property Rights:** legal title to goods or services that confer ownership, possession, control, and the right to exclude other parties from those goods or services.

- **Scarcity**: a situation where a particular good or service cannot be obtained unless a price is paid.

- **Shortage**: when the quantity demanded exceeds the quantity supplied of a particular good or service at a given price.

- **Sunk Cost**: a cost paid in the past that can no longer be recovered or changed.

- **Surplus:** when the quantity demanded falls short of the quantity supplied of a particular good or service at a given price.

- **Transaction Cost:** the cost of facilitating a purchase or sale of a particular good or service in addition to the agreed cost for the actual good or service involved. (for example, the cost of shipping or insuring the actual good).

- **Wealth:** anything that anyone values sufficiently to pay a price to acquire it, or to demand a price for selling it.

About the Author

LES LIVINGSTONE is an MBA Program Director at UMUC (a leading online university). He earned MBA and Ph.D. degrees at Stanford University and is a CPA (licensed in NY and TX). Since 1991 he has directed his own consulting firm which specializes in Damage Estimation for large-scale Commercial Litigation and in Business Valuation. He has served as a Consulting or Testifying Expert in many cases, including Breach of Contract, Patent Infringement, Fraudulent Conveyance, Antitrust, Dealer Termination, Franchise Disputes, and Securities Fraud. He has testified in Federal and State courts in Arizona, California, Florida, Georgia, Illinois, Massachusetts, New York, Rhode Island, and Texas, and he has also testified before committees of the U.S. Congress, U.S. Federal Government agencies including the FTC, FERC, as well as the Public Utilities Commission of Texas.

His previous experience in accounting, finance and business includes the following:

- Babson College: Professor of Accounting and Chairman, Division of Accounting & Law.

- The MAC Group (now Cap Gemini/Ernst & Young Consulting), an international management consulting firm specializing in design and implementation of business strategy for major corporations: Principal.

- Coopers & Lybrand (now PricewaterhouseCoopers), Partner.

- Georgia Institute of Technology: Fuller E. Callaway Professor of Accounting.

- Ohio State University: Arthur Young Distinguished Professor of Accounting.

<u>Publications</u>: Author or coauthor of:

- About 50 articles in leading professional journals.

- Numerous chapters in authoritative handbooks.

- 22 books.

- Recent books include: Some Incomes Are More Equal Than Others (2012), Seen and Unseen (2012), Who is in Charge (2012), Common Sense (2011), Economics Made Easy (2nd Edition, 2011), Finance Made Easy, (2nd Edition, 2011), Ethics Made Easy (2nd Edition, 2011), The Economics of Public Choice (2010), The Economics of Energy (2008), Guide to Business Valuation (2007) and "The Portable MBA in Finance and Accounting", a selection of the Book of the Month Club, the Fortune Book Club and the Money Book Club. Later, the paperback edition was a selection of the Quality Paperback Book Club. Translated into Chinese, French, Indonesian, Japanese, Portuguese, Russian and Spanish. The 4th edition was published in 2009 by John Wiley & Sons, Inc., Hoboken, NJ.

Web Page: http://leslivingstone.com